MW00438484

The ABCs Of Success
And Happiness

DAVE WILLIAMS

The ABCs
Of Success
And
Happiness

DAVE WILLIAMS

The ABCs Of Success And Happiness

Copyright ©2002 by David R. Williams

ISBN   0-938020-64-1

First Printing 2002

Cover Design:
Joe Oberlin & Gerard R. Jones

Published by

DECAPOLIS
PUBLISHING
Printed in the United States of America

BOOKS BY DAVE WILLIAMS

Contents

"Happiness is an inside job."

First Thoughts

The "Luckiest" Person Alive

How lucky are you? Have you won the lottery lately? When was the last time your name was picked in a prize drawing? Have you ever signed up and won the car they were giving away at the grocery store?

Or are you unlucky? Do bad things always happen to you? It rains when you have locked your keys in the car? You get the strange illness no one has ever heard of? Everyone else's food tastes just fine, but yours has a bug in it?

Just how lucky are you?

People who do not know or follow Jesus say they believe in luck — this unseen power that brings good fortune to some people and bad fortune to others. But when you know God through His Son, Jesus

Christ, you believe in something much better than luck. You believe in being blessed. The Bible says:

> The blessing of the LORD makes a person rich, and he adds no sorrow with it.
>
> — Proverbs 10:22 (NLT)
>
> ...Happy indeed are those whose God is the LORD.
>
> — Psalm 144:15b (NLT)

The word "happy" in Hebrew means to be supremely blessed, overflowing with happiness, well-off and prosperous. That means you are "lucky" in every area of life.

God's blessing is a powerful thing, and it is meant for you and me and every other Christian. It is so powerful that it can make rich men out of beggars, and joyful people out of mourners. God can take the fabric of sorrow and turn it into a garment of praise. That is His blessing to us, which is promised in the Word of God, the Bible.

Paul told the Colossians that God wanted them to be fruitful in every good work — successful in every good thing.

> That ye might walk worthy of the Lord unto all pleasing, being fruitful in every good work, and increasing in the knowledge of God;
>
> — Colossians 1:10 (KJV)

Jesus said that God wants to give every good gift to His children.

> If ye then, being evil, know how to give good gifts unto your children, how much more shall your Father which is in heaven give good things to them that ask him?
>
> — Matthew 7:11 (KJV)

James told us that every good gift comes from the Father.

> Every good gift and every perfect gift is from above, and cometh down from the Father of lights, with whom is no variableness, neither shadow of turning.
>
> — James 1:17 (KJV)

So how do we attain the blessing of God? How do we become successful and happy as the Bible promises?

What are the steps? Is it possible to live under God's favor and with His hand upon us?

Yes!

There are simple keys that open the doors of success, prosperity and blessings. There are things you can do right now to start the flow of blessings. I want you to understand them, activate them and live by them.

This book is about God's blessings, and how to have them. I want you to be the "luckiest" person alive, because you are living by God's time-tested principles, obeying Him, walking in the Spirit and enjoying His abundance. You can have success:

- In your job.

- In your family.

- In your spiritual life.

- In your finances.

After a while, your co-workers or friends who don't know the Lord will look at you, shake their heads and say, "You are one lucky person. Your marriage is intact, your kids are great, your finances seem solid, you are healthy and wise. Fate sure is smiling on you."

As if fate were so powerful! No, it is God who gives good things. "Fate" is fickle, but God is faithful, and He rewards believers with much more than we deserve. He will reward you when you begin to put His principles into practice.

This book is for the "lucky" and the "unlucky." Whether it always rains on your parade, or you always win the grand prize, God has something for you. Let's look together at these keys which I call the

"ABCs of Success and Happiness," and let the flow of blessings begin.

Dave Williams

"Keys to success are great, but they are no good without a door."

Chapter One

The Door

Two bums were sitting on a park bench one morning watching the world go by. One leaned over to the other and said, "I had a dream last night that I found the key to success." The other looked at him with wide eyes and asked, "What are you doing with it?" The first answered glumly, "Nothing, I can't find the door!"

Keys to success are great, but they are no good without a door. Before we can talk about the keys to happiness, we need to recognize that Jesus is the Door. All the promises of God's Word come through Him alone.

> **For all the promises of God in Him *are* Yes, and in Him Amen, to the glory of God through us.**
>
> **—2 Corinthians 1:20 (NKJV)**

If you are simply looking for a get-rich-quick scheme or some hocus-pocus business plan, you are in for a surprise. It does not work that way. If you have begun to look for success in the wrong places — perhaps in ungodly teachings, or in dishonorable business practices, or illicit relationships or substances — you, too, are looking in the wrong places with the wrong motives.

You could have a whole janitor's ring of keys, but unless you know the door, you are no better off than if you had no keys at all.

> I am the door: by me if any man enter in, he shall be saved, and shall go in and out, and find pasture.
>
> — John 10:9 (KJV)

I am sure that many of you reading this know the Lord Jesus already, but I also know there are some who do not. Perhaps you were drawn to this book because it talks about success and happiness, two things you may lack in your life. I understand that. Everyone eventually comes to a place where they realize their life is bankrupt without God. It is literally impossible to have lasting success or happiness apart from God. Maybe you have learned that the hard way, but I invite you now to accept Jesus as the door to your freedom and your "ticket" to Heaven. He is the way, the truth and the life, and no one comes to the Father but by Him.

> Jesus saith unto him, I am the way, the truth, and the life: no man cometh unto the Father, but by me.

> — John 14:6 (KJV)

If this is your first time to accept Jesus, or if you are coming back after being away from Him for a while, I encourage you to read another book of mine, *The New Life...The Start Of Something Wonderful.* In fact, this is so important, that I want to send it to you for free. There is an order form in the back of this book. Please call our book store and I will send you this powerful book that will help you get started in a new direction.

I am glad you are taking this journey with me as we discuss how to be successful and happy. That journey begins with Jesus Christ. Having found Him, everything else will begin to fall into place for you.

Power Point Questions:

☐ 1. When did you first meet Jesus?

☐ 2. How has He changed your life?

"Use the seed you have to produce the crop you want."

Chapter Two

The First Key

There I was in the St. Louis airport, my luggage weighing heavier by the minute, people streaming by me to make their connecting flights, and business-men parked in the waiting areas with their laptop computers and cellular phones. An ill-timed thunderstorm in Detroit had forced my plane to sit on the runway for two hours, and I had missed my connecting flight in St. Louis to Tulsa.

Now, in the bustle of the airport, my options were growing thin. I was on a split ticket, meaning I flew on two different airlines, and neither one felt particularly responsible for my situation because they did not coordinate their schedules together. Concern began to creep over me as I considered my options.

Should I spend the night in St. Louis?

Rent a car and drive the remaining eight hours?

Stand-by on a later flight?

Mosey around the airport for hours until the air-lines solve my problem?

Then I realized I had another option, the best one of all. I could choose my reaction. Instead of think-ing, "Woe is me," I could roll with the punches. So what if I had to spend the night in St. Louis? What was so bad about that? I would get in a day late, but it would not kill me. I remembered the story of the 100-year-old man who was asked for the secret of his longevity. He said, "Never run for a bus. There will always be another one."

I decided to praise the Lord. I said, "God, You are so good! At least I got this far and even if I have to rent a car, it is only an eight-hour drive to Tulsa from St. Louis. That will give me time to pray." I walked up to the ticket counter and explained my situation, then handed the agent my cheap ticket. She said, "Mr. Williams, there is only one seat left on the next flight to Tulsa and it is a First Class seat, so we will be happy to give it to you."

In an instant, my whole situation turned around; but really, my outlook had turned around already when I decided to accept what had happened and be happy anyway. Nothing the agent could have said would have disappointed me.

The "A" Of The ABCs

The Lord was teaching me a lesson that day in the airport: When we accept responsibility for our own success and happiness, we open ourselves to greater blessings, along with the favor of God and man.

That is the first key. Are you ready?

A = ACCEPT responsibility for your own success and happiness.

Do not wait for your ship to come in. Do not wait until you win the lottery to be happy. Do not wait for somebody else to make you successful, because somebody else won't. Do not wait to find two thousand dollars under a rock to pay your bills, or for God to mysteriously provide an unmarked envelope with the cash you have been asking Him for.

Accept responsibility for your own success, your own happiness, your own application of the precious promises that God has given to all believers. As soon as you do, you'll find yourself saying something like this: "I will apply faith to the promises of God. I am **not** going to wait for the pastor to do it, the deacon to do it, the Sunday school teacher to do it, the usher to do it. I am **not** going to wait for my husband or wife or children to make me happy. I am **not** going to wait for the situation to make me happy. I am **not** going to wait for anything to make me happy. I **am** going to be happy, period, because the promises I have in Christ are so good, I have no reason to be anything but happy."

You see, happiness is an inside job. It is decided by internal factors, not external ones. Have you noticed how glum people seem to want to stay glum? If a person is unhappy, nobody can make him or her happy. An unhappy wife will look to her husband to make her happy and wonder why he doesn't. An unhappy husband will look to his wife to make him happy and wonder why she doesn't. In truth, they have decided to *not* be happy.

You can decide to be happy and successful even in the worst of conditions. Think of Joseph, sold into slavery by his brothers. He made a decision that he was not going to take offense and nurture his grudge against them. He accepted responsibility for his own happiness and success, and in a few years he became Prime Minister of Egypt. You see, something supernatural happens when we say, "God, you have given me the promises, you have given me the blood of Jesus, you have given me angels as my ministering servants, you have given me everything that I need. I am going to accept responsibility and apply these promises to my life, my business, my marriage, my family. I am going after it! I **am** going to be supremely blessed! *Nothing* is going to stop that."

The Choice Is Ours

Here is a surprise: The vast majority of unsuccessful, unhappy people are that way *not* because they lack ability or talent, but because they are unwilling to accept responsibility.

What would you think of a man who sat in front of a fireplace and cursed it for not giving him heat, but who was not willing to put the logs next to him in the fireplace and light them with the matches in his pocket? You would say he is either crazy or lazy. God gave him logs, matches and a fireplace. What more was there for Him to do? Send heavenly flames into the man's home? A man like that misunderstands how God works. God grew the tree that provided the wood and created the sulfur that was made into matches. Now it is time for the man to do his part.

When you and I begin to accept responsibility for our own happiness and accept responsibility for our own success, something happens. We join a minority. We no longer think like the masses, the people who constantly feel victimized. When somebody hurts them or does them wrong, they give away the key to their happiness and success. They put the responsibility on somebody else and forfeit the destiny God has designed for them.

Sometimes this happens to me. I have a tendency to let nasty comments bother me. The poisoned words start eating me up. I think about it and try to pray about it, but my mind keeps going back to the offense. Only by accepting my own response can I break free of the cycle of unhappiness. God teaches me that He will keep me in perfect peace if I keep my mind upon Him and accept responsibility.

> Thou wilt keep *him* in perfect peace, *whose* mind *is* stayed *on thee*: because he trusteth in thee.
>
> — Isaiah 26:3 (KJV)

> Peace I leave with you, my peace I give unto you: not as the world giveth, give I unto you. Let not your heart be troubled, neither let it be afraid.
>
> — John 14:27 (KJV)

I am not a victim, and neither are you. We are more than conquerors, able to do all things through Christ who gives us strength.

> Nay, in all these things we are more than conquerors through him that loved us.
>
> — Romans 8:37 (KJV)

> I can do all things through Christ which strengtheneth me.
>
> — Philippians 4:13 (KJV)

Sowing Seeds Of Responsibility

Responsibility is a powerful tool. The parable Jesus told about the talents is largely about responsibility.

I recently heard a radio report with rather shocking statistics. The reporter said that in homes where dads refuse to accept their responsibilities, the children are fifty percent more likely to commit suicide, seventy-eight percent more likely to commit a serious crime, and seventy percent more likely to spend time in prison. Daughters are sixty percent more likely to become pregnant without being married, and far more likely to contract a sexually transmitted disease.

What a high price to pay for irresponsible fathering! Even in cases where a marriage breaks up, the study found that if a dad will continue to support and keep in contact with the children, the percentages go significantly down for suicides and crime.

Use The Seed You Have To Produce The Crop You Want

Accepting responsibility for our own success and happiness is one of the most powerful things we can do, and it affects other people and determines the course of our own lives. Many of the blessings I am experiencing today are the results of seeds that my wife and I sowed years ago. We use the seed we have to produce the crop we want, and God continues to bring great increase. Imagine a farmer who does not sow seeds, then stands on the edge of the field yelling, "Grow, crops! Give me a harvest."

The ground yells back, "You haven't planted anything!"

In harvest season only weeds will appear in those fields, because something will grow in the fertile soil, and only we decide what that is.

> While the earth remaineth, seedtime and harvest...
>
> — Genesis 8:22a (KJV)

Our lives are the same — fertile soil intended to grow ever-increasing crops. If we do not plant good seeds into the soil, then unwanted weeds — thoughts, habits and deeds — will grow there instead. In fact, look at your life today. Do you see weeds or a fruitful crop? Is your yield worthy of the storehouse or the bonfire?

Today, your condition and mine is the result of seeds we planted yesterday. Our level of happiness and success today was shaped by our attitudes and actions of yesterday. If you have a small harvest now, take heart. You can always begin a new season by accepting responsibility and planting new seeds right now that will yield results for you in the future.

Do you want a big harvest tomorrow? Plant the right seeds today. Plant attitude seeds, success seeds, happiness seeds. The conditions are always right to begin planting. Do not wait for a vacation from work, or a better job offer, or for your kids to leave or your spouse to die. A minute delayed is a minute wasted because God begins growing those seeds the moment we plant them.

Miss America

One of my heroes is Cheryl Salem, the former Miss America from Mississippi. As a little girl, her trust and confidence were torn apart when she was abused and mistreated by a close relative. Not only that, but everything seemed to be against her. She was from a poor family in a poor town in Mississippi, the poorest state in the Union. Anyone looking into that little girl's smudged face would have said she was trapped, but Cheryl had an inner determination that transcended her circumstances — and she wanted to be Miss America so she could tell people about her faith in Jesus.

But the dream was shattered when, at the age of twelve, she was in a brutal car accident that seemed to steal her dream forever. Her little body flew through the windshield, and the glass tore up her innocent, cherubic face. As a result of the accident, one leg was shattered and grew in shorter than the other, so she walked with a limp. Scarred, half-crippled, Cheryl could have thrown in the towel, but she didn't. Instead she realized that if she was going to have a shot at being Miss America, she'd have to take responsibility. She asked God what she had to do to get her leg to the right length. She'd never seen anybody limp down the Miss America runway. The Lord led her to Mark 11:23-24 which talks about speaking to mountains and having faith and not doubting, and so she began to proclaim that God was going to heal her. She took those verses to heart and meditated on them, and God began to re-write her future.

> For verily I say unto you, That whosoever shall say unto this mountain, Be thou removed, and be thou cast into the sea; and shall not doubt in his heart, but shall believe that those things which he saith shall come to pass; he shall have whatsoever he saith. Therefore I say unto you, What things soever ye desire, when ye pray, believe that ye receive *them*, and ye shall have *them*.
>
> — Mark 11:23-24 (KJV)

She heard about an evangelist coming to a nearby town, and that night she went to his meeting and was miraculously healed! But that was only the first step. Cheryl worked her way through college and began entering pageants. She was still so innocent and un-practiced that she knew nothing about buying thou-sand-dollar gowns. So she and her sister bought $50 worth of fabric and paid a seamstress $15 to make a dress, and then they sat at the kitchen table and glued sequins and pearls on it! In that dress she won Miss Mississippi, walking very carefully across the plat-form so the sequins and pearls didn't pop off!

You see, because she accepted the responsibility, God provided the promises. It was up to her to go after those promises, do what she could do, and be-lieve God for what she couldn't do. She moved on to the Miss America pageant, and with the help of an-other dress made by the seamstress for $15, Cheryl Prewitt (now Salem) from Mississippi — that mis-treated little girl who'd been in a car accident but re-fused to let life steal her dream — won the Miss America crown! As the crowd applauded and the victory music played, she smiled and waved and walked down the runway knowing that God had worked a miracle in her life.

She used her year as Miss America to tell people about Jesus. The Miss America committee even told her that they were looking forward to the next year because they were so tired of hearing about Jesus!

Cheryl is a sterling example of someone who ac-cepted responsibility for her own success and happiness. God has given every one of us everything we need to be a major, smashing, successful, victorious believer and to lead a happy life. He has given us His divine nature to work in us to achieve the dreams He gives us.

> **His divine power has given us everything we need for life and godliness through our knowledge of him...**
>
> — **2 Peter 1:3a**

This divine power works in everyone who has come to Christ.

> **Now to him who is able to do immeasurably more than all we ask or imagine, according to his power that is at work in us.**
>
> — **Ephesians 3:20**

This divine power is working in every believer! It was at work in Cheryl's life, and that divine power is at work in you as a Christian.

Power Point Questions:

☐ 1. Are there areas in which you have given up responsibility? What are they?

☐ 2. How can you take responsibility for your success and happiness right now?

☐ 3. How do you want your life to be different in six months?

"God sees you and me very differently than we usually see ourselves."

Chapter Three

The Second Key

What do you see when you close your eyes? What images and dreams flicker and flash through your mind? Cheryl saw images of herself winning the Miss America pageant. Athletes and other competitive people say they visualize their entire contest before actually competing. They see themselves making big plays, and holding the trophy at the end.

The second key to success and happiness is this:

B = BE a big dreamer!

God has put within every believer the divine nature to see things that we do not see in the natural, and to call things that are not as though they are.

> (As it is written, I have made thee a father of many nations,) before him whom he believed, *even* God, who quickeneth the dead, and cal-

leth those things which be not as though they
were.

— Romans 4:17 (KJV)

That means that we can, by faith declare our
God-given dreams before they become real in the
physical world. This type of declaration has power
with God.

This principle has been foundational in my own
life, and I go back to it when I find myself overwork-
ing and coming near the edge of stress. I learned it at
a conference in Buffalo, New York, from a South Ko-
rean pastor named David Yonggi Cho. Cho told us
he used to preach with his eyes closed at his church
in Seoul. A lady one day asked him why, and he answered, "With my eyes open I see only a handful of
people in the church. With my eyes closed, I see the
place full." Cho was seeing things that were not as
though they were.

At the time he spoke to us, Cho's church already
had 100,000 members. Today, his church has 800,000
members. When he began thirty years ago, the coun-
try was Buddhist by a vast majority. Today the majority of South Korea is Christian!

Cho's vision, which was really God's vision, came
to pass, and a crucial factor was that he visualized
and believed the dream he had in his heart.

You want to be successful? Happy? Be a big dreamer. Dreaming — seeing something by faith — is a spiritual principle that you cannot afford to neglect. It will mean the difference between attaining your dreams, or going a lifetime without attaining them.

Occultists have tried to steal this principle from God's people. Many have maligned and ridiculed it. But Paul said:

> So we fix our eyes not on what is seen, but on what is unseen. For what is seen is temporary, but what is unseen is eternal.
>
> — 2 Corinthians 4:18

Self-vision

The Bible is full of wonderful descriptions of God's people — you and me. Throughout the New Testament we are called God's workmanship, His chosen people, the sons and daughters of God. We are forgiven, redeemed, made holy and set apart for good works. When I read all these things, I almost feel overwhelmed at how gracious God has been to me.

Why does He say all those things about us? First of all, they are true. Second of all, God wants to elevate our self-vision — the inner picture of ourselves.

Some of you may say, "I am really having a struggle. I do not feel like the righteousness of God right now."

But do you know what God said about us as believers? He said we are saints if we have come to Christ. He said we are ministers and ambassadors of Christ.

> But in all *things* approving ourselves as the ministers of God, in much patience, in afflictions, in necessities, in distresses,
>
> — 2 Corinthians 6:4 (KJV)

> Now then we are ambassadors for Christ, as though God did beseech *you* by us: we pray *you* in Christ's stead, be ye reconciled to God.
>
> — 2 Corinthians 5:20 (KJV)

Jesus said, "I am the Light of the world," (John 8:12) then said to His followers, "You are the light of the world" (Matthew 5:14). He said, "Nothing will be impossible for you."

> .... and nothing shall be impossible unto you.
>
> — Matthew 17:20c (KJV)

Many of the things Jesus said about Himself, He also said about His people.

Of course, we do not presume on who He is. He is Christ. Paul said we are the body of Christ (Romans 12:4-5). We have only one Savior. Only *He* died on the cross for us.

But most of the things Jesus said about Himself, He said about His Church as well. That means you and I are saints, ministers, ambassadors, and the light of the world!

We Rise To The Level Of Our Inner Vision

It seems to me that much of the work of God is getting His people to believe who they are in Him. We rise to the level of how we see ourselves. Jesus saw the disciples not as smelly fishermen but as world-changers. Think of the kid who grows up hearing, "You are a loser. You will never amount to anything." Soon he starts telling himself the same thing, and eventually his life bears it out, unless God gets hold of him first.

God sees you and me very differently than we usually see ourselves. Remember Gideon, the man who led a tiny army of Israelites against a much bigger army, and won a great victory? After his men hid their lamps in pots, they smashed the pots and surprised the enemy! That was all well and good, but our first view of Gideon was as a skinny runt stomping on grapes. He did not have a dream of being a deliverer. He saw himself as being the least in his whole family. But God told an angel to go to Gideon and announce something entirely different. So an angel showed up while Gideon was stomping the grapes and said, "Hello, Gideon, you mighty man of valor," and Gideon said, "Not me, I am the least in my family." The angel had to keep reaffirming, "You are a mighty man of valor," until Gideon got the picture, the vision, the dream of himself as a mighty man of valor. (See Judges chapter 6.)

Before God could use Gideon, he had to elevate his self-vision. I am convinced He does the same for you and me.

Church-vision

Our limitless God is limited in our lives when we do not dream big. When I first took the pastorate of Mount Hope Church in Lansing, Michigan, where I am pastor today, the church had 226 people. When I became pastor, it went down a little bit in attendance. I remember praying at 5:30 in the morning, "God, I want to have a successful church," and I remembered what Cho said: "You have got to see it." The book of Proverbs put it this way:

> Where *there is* no vision, the people perish...
>
> — Proverbs 29:18a (KJV)

Without having a dream, a vision, something born in the heart of God that you can **see**, God's people fail and perish. So I started saying, "God, I see it. I see this 450-seat church full of people worshiping You and learning week after week."

I was reading my Bible one day and I came upon Acts 13:44, a verse I had read many times, but this time it stood out, as if with neon lights. It said:

> The following week almost the entire city turned out to hear them preach the word of the Lord.
>
> — Acts 13:44 (NLT)

I thought, "Almost the whole city! Wow, that is a good goal."

I closed my eyes and said, "Lord, I see the ushers setting up chairs every week." In a matter of months, in that 450-seat church, we were cramming in 475 people and the ushers were setting up extra rows of chairs. It got to the point where people were sitting on air conditioners. We had to disband the choir so people could sit in the choir risers to get into church. Police were calling us because, on occasion, traffic was backing up all the way to the highway.

An out-of-town family was visiting Lansing and went to the Christian book store at one of the malls asking about a good church to attend. The cashier said, "Try Mount Hope Church. I don't go there, but everybody else in town does."

I saw how powerful the principle of visualizing and dreaming was, and started using it to propel us toward other goals. I told the congregation, "Close your eyes. I want you to see us giving one million dollars to world missions, feeding the hungry, help-ing children in orphanages and winning souls in cru-sades. See the mercury in the thermometer breaking out the top at the one million dollar mark." The people were clapping and cheering, even though we were giving only $35,000 at the time. I also told them, "See a 3,000-seat worship center."

I will always remember when a deacon put his arm around me and said, "Now, you are just a young dreamer. You had better quit getting people's hopes up, because when it does not come to pass, you are going to lose a lot of credibility." I am glad I never listened to that deacon! The Mount Hope Church fam-ily has grown to ten thousand, and we were able to give three million dollars to missions this year.

I believe in getting people's hopes up, because if people do not get their hopes up, their faith cannot get up either, because faith is the substance of things hoped for.

> **Now faith is the substance of things hoped for,**
> **the evidence of things not seen.**
>
> **— Hebrews 11:1 (KJV)**

Hope must be present before faith can be acti-vated. Some people say, "Don't get your hopes up." I say, "I am going to get my hopes up as high as I can!" Oral Roberts had a plaque on his desk that said,

"Make no small plans here." I agree with that. God is interested in increase. He is interested in making your dream come true.

But you have to have a dream first.

I have learned not to dream according to my wallet, because my wallet is never big enough, and I will never have, at any given moment, enough money to carry out God's dream for me.

The first time you dream something, the thought will come, "How are you going to pay for it? Who is going to help you? People will think you are crazy." When you are in the dream phase on your road to success and happiness, do not worry about how it is going to come to pass.

I still don't know how God is going to get my whole city saved, discipled, and into church. I don't have to know. I can just dream it and God will take me there step by step.

Our church has tackled many things that did not seem reasonable when we started. We decided to include a healing center, medical and dental clinic within our new facilities. God gave us a plan to keep planting, establishing and growing churches, even though many churches in the U.S. are in decline.

Three or four years ago, my wife, Mary Jo and I launched a missions ministry to provide scholarships for African students who have the fire of God burning in their bellies, but cannot afford Bible school or seminary. Our scholarships put them through Bible school. Today, nearly all of them are in full-time ministry, winning souls for Jesus, and changing their nations. I saw how investing in people can change things, but it would not have happened the way it did if my wife and I had not dreamed beyond our capabilities.

Not By Might

Harry, who was not a very religious man, came down with cancer. He found a piece of literature by an evangelist that talked about faith and vision. Harry knew he was going to die, so he decided to take a gamble on God, and said a simple prayer. "God, you know I have not paid much attention to you over the years, I have not felt like I have needed you, but now I don't know what to do. I read this article and it tells me I can come to Jesus. Lord, forgive me for all the ways I have ignored you. And Lord, please help me to defeat this cancer."

Harry was already in bad shape. He could not eat. He was growing thinner and thinner, and when he tried to eat, he would gag. But he started visualizing things with his eye of faith that he could not see in the natural. He started picturing little cells dressed up like army men, complete with grenades and guns, who went marching into his body, and whenever they came upon a cell that was harmful, he saw them blow up that cell. Then another group of soldiers came in and carried out that cell. For three weeks he did this. After three weeks, he regained his appetite and started eating and gaining weight. He went back for tests and the doctors told him his cancer was nowhere to be found.

Harry had a God-given dream, and he visualized it and then watched it come to pass. Did he do it in the natural energies of his flesh? No, he did it by the Spirit of God, by dreaming a big dream and calling those things which were not as though they were.

But there is an important principle yet to be learned about being a big dreamer. When we want to be successful, the first thing we normally do is swing into action and try to make it happen. We are told by the world that we are responsible for our success and happiness, and for the dreams we have. But the Bible gives a totally different principle.

Nothing lasting is ever achieved with natural energies or natural dreams. In Zechariah 4:6, the priest was wondering how he was going to build a temple, and God spoke and said:

> Not by might, nor by power, but by my spirit, saith the LORD of hosts.
>
> — Zechariah 4:6c (KJV)

Partnering With God

Dreams are a partnership. We allow them to take root, we work toward them and picture them happening, and the Spirit of the Lord does the work we cannot do. He also energizes us with divine energy. You find it happening step by step, almost like a miracle, not in the natural energies of ourselves, but by the Spirit of God!

I remember the day years ago when the pepper spray shipment I had bought leaked all over my garage. I had boxes of the stuff and was trying to sell it to make money. I had seen an advertisement in the newspaper that said, "Protect yourself with pepper spray. Become a distributor." The manufacturer sold them to salesmen for a few dollars per squirt bottle, and the salesmen sold them for much more. I figured I could start another income stream in addition to the other businesses I had.

I learned firsthand with that pepper spray and on numerous other occasions how silly it is to do things in the flesh. I used to see ads that said, "Make $10,000 an hour in your spare time! Call this toll-free number and send $79.95 for the course." At one point I sold last wills and testaments kits that people could fill out themselves. I advertised them in the newspaper with a line that said, "Don't die without a will."

I spent more money on the advertising and printing of those wills than I ever made back through purchases.

So in the natural energies of the flesh, it never worked. Of course, that was not God's destiny for me, to sell wills or pepper spray.

The Galatians had started out well in their service of the Lord, but then Paul said they became hypnotized or bewitched. In Galatians he said:

> Paul, an apostle—sent not from men nor by man, but by Jesus Christ and God the Father, who raised him from the dead—
>
> — Galatians 1:1
>
> Are you so foolish? After beginning with the Spirit, are you now trying to attain your goal by human effort?
>
> — Galatians 3:3

A naturally energized dream is no dream at all, because anything born of the flesh will eventually die, and true dreams never die.

Many Christians go through life without direction, as if clicking away with a camera without bothering to focus. "Hey, no time to focus," they say. "I have just got to take these pictures." Then when the pictures come out, they are blurry and unusable. You have wasted time, money, and energy because you did not focus. Having a dream gives us focus.

If you are in Christ, you have a host of promises. God has a dream for your life. It is time to set those small dreams aside and let the big ones take hold.

Take a moment and think. Are there dreams hiding in your heart that you have not allowed to grow? What have you always wanted to do? What has God spoken to you about doing? What has stopped you?

Now take charge! Dream big, and let God surprise you as you go after them. We will see how He does that in coming chapters.

Power Point Questions:

☐ 1. What dreams do you have for yourself?

☐ 2. What dreams do you have for your church?

☐ 3. Make a list of the three most important things you want to accomplish in the next ten years.

"When faced with a mountain, we can either stop altogether because it looms too big, or we can believe that the mountain was put there to challenge us to reach higher and to believe the promise of God to fulfill our dream."

Chapter Four

The Third Key

I knew a little boy named Davie who was always building roller coasters, airplanes and helicopters. He wanted so badly to fly. His mother would look out the back window and see him jumping off the roof, sometimes with an umbrella, or a sheet with ropes tied to it, or even big foam pieces strapped to his arms.

One day he bought some lightweight wood and turned his bicycle into an airplane with wings and a tail. He rode as fast as he could down the street, but it would not lift off, so he decided to ride it down a hill to build up more speed and launch it off the ground. He convinced the neighbor boy to be the test pilot for the dangerous mission, and instructed him to pedal as fast as he could while Davie pushed him down the hill. They counted down from ten and then started going, and sure enough the bike started to lift off, but only the front wheel, and just enough so the neighbor boy could not steer. He screamed as he barreled into a grove of pine trees, smashing off the wings. He survived, and Davie went on to try many other attempts at flight.

I know. I was Davie.

The challenges of flying did not stop my young mind from trying. In fact, parents, you never have to worry about kids who are always inventing something, taking things apart and getting into mischief. If you have a child who is always doing something crazy, do not worry — that kid will go places. You have to worry about the one who doesn't have any dreams or ambitions, and is lethargic. The mischievous ones may need direction, but they do not need a cattle prod to get them moving!

Now that I am an adult, the same principle holds true from when I was a boy. When faced with a mountain, we can either stop altogether because it looms too big, or we can believe that the mountain was put there to challenge us to reach higher and to believe the promise of God to fulfill our dream. As an adult I worked hard and earned my pilot's license. No more jumping off roofs for me!

You know you are on your way toward your dream when the road is full of challenges.

That leads us to the third key. So far we have:

A = Accept responsibility for your success and happiness.

B = Be a big dreamer.

Now C:

C = CHALLENGE yourself to new heights.

A dream will not come easily. Funny that the stereotypical "dreamer" is someone who thinks but never acts. True dreamers are people who think, and then act, despite the hardships. No dream comes to pass without major challenges. When we meet these challenges, we challenge ourselves to higher heights and greater accomplishments.

The Man Who Never Gave Up

There is a story in the Bible that I absolutely love. It is in the book of Numbers, chapter 13. Moses sent twelve spies into the land God had promised to the children of Israel. The spies spent forty days there, checking it out so they could bring a report to the rest of the nation. When they came back, ten of them spoke negatively about the promised land and purposefully struck terror in the hearts of the people. They said:

> ...We went into the land to which you sent us, and it does flow with milk and honey! Here is

> its fruit. But the people who live there are pow-
> erful, and the cities fortified and very large....
>
> — Numbers 13:27-28a

Later their report got even worse, verses 32b and 33b:

> ...The land we explored devours those living in it. All the people we saw there are of great size. ... We seemed like grasshoppers in our own eyes, and we looked the same to them.

They started seeing the promised land as a handicap instead of a challenge.

But there was a dreamer in the bunch, and his name was Caleb. He could not stand all the negativity, so he stilled the people and said in verse 30:

> We should go up and take possession of the land, for we can certainly do it.

Caleb had great faith. Later in life, when he was eighty years old, he told the people he still felt like a forty-year-old. He was still conquering mountains, and his whole family was blessed as a result. He did not see problems as handicaps. He saw them as challenges to overcome.

But Caleb, along with his friend Joshua, who also had great faith, were drowned out by the voices of doubt. Verse 31 says:

> But the men who had gone up with him said,
> "We can't attack those people; they are stronger
> than we are."

Ten of them saw the size of the people as an insurmountable handicap. Two of them saw it as a challenge God had set before them. And among those twelve spies, only two, Joshua and Caleb got to go into the promise land. The others perished.

These stories in the Old Testament are for our good. We ought to realize that every difficulty we face is an opportunity. We can overcome it and possess the promises of God, or we can get knocked out of the game.

A Way Of Life

When you challenge yourself to believe the promises of God, you will find you can beat the odds — every time. Someone once said that you, plus God equals a majority. That is certainly true. When you challenge yourself to new levels of faith you will run faster than you have ever run; climb higher than you have ever climbed; achieve more than you thought possible.

Is this getting through to you? It is not just a pep talk — it is a way of life, one that has been proven throughout the Bible and is still being proven by men and women of faith.

There was a man named W. Page Pitt, who faced a major life challenge. People said Pitt should have failed, but he succeeded. When he was five years old, he started going blind and eventually lost ninety-seven percent of his eyesight. His parents, however, refused to put him in a school for the blind. They determined, "You are going to learn to do everything a sighted child does. This is not a handicap, Page. This is a challenge."

So Page went to school, and he learned. He took oral exams instead of written exams. He listened to books on tape. He did not just do the bare minimum, but went searching for challenges. He went to college and earned his undergraduate degree. He continued on to graduate school and earned his graduate degree. He became Dr. Page Pitt, journalist. He eventually became the head of the Journalism Department at Marshall University.

One day, an insensitive student came up to him and asked, "Dr. Pitt, could you tell me what your worst handicap is?" Dr. Pitt thought for a moment, because he knew the student was referring to his blindness; but Pitt never saw his blindness as a handicap. He replied, "Young man, I want to tell you something. Blindness is not a handicap. Being physically challenged is not a handicap, unless you let it be a handicap. The real handicaps in life are lethargy, ir-responsibility, and lack of ambition and desire."

That brings me to the three points I believe are essential to overcoming the challenges we face.

• *Point Number One: Strong Commitment*

There are those who will come to church, watch Gospel programs, listen to Gospel radio broadcasts, but tip toe around making a commitment to Christ. They say, "Religion is good, but to each his own."

I am a baby boomer, and one thing my generation did not talk about much is commitment. We were selfish, the "me-generation," and we did not care about leaving a legacy of commitment for future generations. We believed in having different spouses for different phases of life, and dreamed of self-fulfillment, self-realization and self-help, but threw commitment right out the door.

We knew nothing about commitment, so we taught nothing about commitment.

Little did we know that with God we can have all that we need right now, and leave a legacy of commitment that will honor our memory.

Indeed, commitment is like a secret roadmap to success and happiness. The longer we are committed to one spouse, the better it gets. The longer we are committed to Christ and to serving the Church, the better our lives get because God rewards us.

The first step in overcoming a challenge is to commit to overcoming it. At that moment, supernatural power kicks in, and you can expect one surprise after another as God helps you toward your goal. Commitment is not saying, "I will see how it works out." It is saying, "I am putting my hand to the plow, looking straight ahead, moving forward, facing this challenge, and nothing will stop me." That is when God moves in, infusing you with divine strength.

I remember sitting in a church service almost thirty years ago, listening to Sister Rosalta Fisher who had been a missionary, a pastor, and evangelist. I was struggling with whether or not God had called me into the full-time ministry and her words rang out like a clarion call to me. She did not walk much on the platform because she was advanced in years, but it was like power coming out of every word she said. She said, "Some of you are like big ships. You have the power to be out to sea, to go places, to do big things, yet you are tied to the pier. It is time to cut the ropes and launch out into the deep! You will never know what you can do, if you stay tied to the pier."

It hit my heart, and I said a great big "Yes!" on the inside. I had a job that I enjoyed. I had advanced rapidly, and was satisfied with my paycheck. But after that service I turned in my resignation and started on the path toward full-time ministry. I accepted the challenge God had given me through His servant, Rosalta Fisher.

Does the name Scott Hamilton ring a bell to you? Scott won the hearts and admiration of the world at the 1984 Olympics in Sarajevo, where he won the gold medal in the ice skating competition. What many people did not know was that when Scott was two years old, he developed a childhood disease that left him stunted. He did not grow. He overcame that disease, but he was always smaller than his classmates. He had been adopted, and his adoptive parents thought that teaching him to skate might help his rehabilitation. They told him to view his problem as a challenge, not a handicap, and that made the difference in Scott's life.

• *Point Number Two: The Law Of "Little By Little"*

I like to buy logs of summer sausage. I can't eat a whole sausage at once, but after a week of eating little slices here and there, it disappears and I can't believe I ate the whole thing. That is how we move ahead in God. Often we see as the ten spies saw: The task is too big. The mountain is too high. The challenge is too great.

Once we have committed to overcoming a challenge, it is still possible to be overwhelmed by its size, and that is why we need to follow the biblical pattern of overcoming it little by little. God said to His people:

> The LORD your God will drive out those nations before you, little by little. You will not be allowed to eliminate them all at once, or the wild animals will multiply around you.
>
> — Deuteronomy 7:22

How were they to do it? Little by little, over time.

Every mountain can be torn down, if you have the faith to move one rock at a time. Even better is that within the law of little by little is the law of supernatural intervention. Just as God rewards true commitment with divine intervention, He rewards our little efforts with big ones. When we start removing the mountain one rock at a time, God will send an earthquake to send it crumbling down. He will move Heaven and earth for people who walk by faith.

That is how it was with the twelve disciples of Jesus. He told them to go out, heal the sick, cleanse the lepers, cast out devils and preach the kingdom. They did not feel overwhelmed by the task, and they did not try to have mass crusades and get the job done in one fell swoop. They met the challenge person by person, healing this one, then that one, preaching to this one, then that one. Crusades are terrific, but when you are just starting out, ministry is more about being faithful with the small numbers you have, rather than the large numbers you don't.

Later, Jesus gave quite an astounding commission to the Church: Go into *all the world* and preach the Gospel. Make disciples of every nation. Did they shrink back from that mountain? There were only one hundred and twenty of them on the day of Pentecost. They owned no radio or television stations, had no jets or fax machines, cell phones, e-mail or printing presses. How did Jesus expect them to go into all the world and preach the Gospel?

The answer is this: Little by little. When we meet the challenge God sets before us, He supernaturally works through our efforts. Those one hundred and twenty people started out in Jerusalem, then Judea, then Samaria and then the uttermost parts of the earth, and in thirty-one years, the entire known world had heard the Gospel of Jesus Christ.

There are people in my congregation who have done extraordinary things like earning college degrees while working full-time and running a family. They did it by taking one class at a time, tackling it semester by semester and not becoming over-whelmed.

I did the same thing with my undergraduate and graduate degrees. Even though I was working full-time, I studied long hours to get my Bible and doc-trinal diploma and then my ministerial diploma. It was twenty-two years from the time I graduated from high school to the time I earned an undergraduate degree. It took seven more years to earn my gradu-ate degree. I could have dismissed the idea of fur-ther education because my plate was full. I had a church to run, a family to guide, a job to do, but by employing the law of little by little, I cut that moun-tain down to size.

When I started learning to fly, it was like walking blindfolded through a maze because pilots always talk in initials. They will say, "Did you call the FSS? We are going to have to call the ATC once we get about 500 AGL." I heard this chatter and did not know what they were talking about. I wondered how I would ever remember all the terms. But, like any pilot, I eventually did learn them, and now when other pilots talk about an FBO or AGL or MSL, I under-stand.

I did it little by little, and so can you with what-ever mountain you are facing.

• *Point Number Three: Let God Infuse You With Power*

The third point is simple. Do your best and commit the rest to God. He is the one who has promised to infuse us with strength through His Son Jesus Christ.

There is an often-quoted passage in Philippians 4:13 that reads:

> I can do all things through Christ which strengtheneth me.
>
> — Philippians 4:13 (KJV)

Another translation says we can do all things through Him who "infuses inner strength" into us.

Infusion — it means to pour in, to soak, to fill, to impart. It is like putting a tea bag in hot water, and all of a sudden the tea permeates the water. Paul is saying that Christ's strength in him became equal to and greater than anything he faced — and he faced a lot.

The divine infusion of power is what will propel us past the challenges we face; not our own commitment, no matter how valiant, and not our own work, even if we do it little by little. Only God's power can make the difference. Remember the verse?

> ...Not by might, nor by power, but by my spirit, saith the LORD of hosts.
>
> — Zechariah 4:6c (KJV)

Is there an area of your life where God is telling you to launch out into the deep? Jesus did not say to tiptoe through the tulips. He did not say to wade in the shallow. He said to launch out into the deep. Take a risk. Dare to do something big with your life. Challenge yourself to do it, trusting in the infusing power of Jesus Christ working in you.

So have courage! These little challenges we face, and even the bigger ones we wish we could avoid, are preparing us for greater things ahead. If we do not meet the challenges, and if we do not challenge ourselves, trusting the promises of God and the infusion of His power, we will not be ready for the next challenge. God may have something designed wonderful for us ahead, but we must overcome our present challenges to get there.

There is great reward for those who do. There was a fellow I knew who was at one time in management at a major university in Michigan. Then his boss retired, leaving an open position that required a different kind of degree than he had. The university searched for somebody to fill the position, and in the meantime asked the fellow to pick up the workload. He could have said, "I don't want more responsibility. I don't want more oversight. You guys don't pay me enough, and I am hurt that you won't offer me the job." Instead, he accepted the challenge. He knew that the power and strength of Christ was infused into his life, and that would help him overcome.

He started delegating more tasks to secretaries, re-training people and re-structuring the way work was done. He saved the university lots of money, and was essentially filling two management positions. Recognizing this, they created a special position for him and gave him a big pay raise.

You can take on a challenge, whatever it is. It may be to bring somebody to church who doesn't normally come. Maybe you are working on an invention that might change the world.

> **I wisdom dwell with prudence, and find out knowledge of witty inventions.**
>
> — Proverbs 8:12 (KJV)

Maybe God wants to give you a witty invention to bless the world. What if you had started the Internet? What if you developed software that vastly improved people's lives?

You say, "That could never happen to me." Why not?

I think of Bob Carlisle, the man who wrote the hit song "Butterfly Kisses." He blessed the world with his witty invention and became popular practically overnight with a song written for his daughter. The song touched the hearts of millions.

God wants to do that with you, too. If you will challenge yourself to reach higher heights, to do more than you can do, achieve more than you can achieve, and rely on His infusion of power to overcome the mountains.

Challenge yourself, and see what God can do! I challenge you right now to launch out in at least two areas of your life, whether in volunteering, education, career or something else you have been thinking and dreaming about. Make a measurable change, and then brace yourself for the infusion of God's power that is sure to come.

Power Point Questions:

☐ 1. What challenges do you face right now?

☐ 2. When was the last time you challenged yourself to a higher place in God?

☐ 3. Choose one thing you can do immediately to move ahead in your job, your family and your walk with Christ.

Chapter Five

Spiritual Flubber

Making a strong commitment to the things of God and the challenges of our dreams is one step toward success and happiness. The next is to develop unconquerable determination to follow through with that commitment.

> *A = Accept responsibility for your own success and happiness.*

> *B = Be a big dreamer.*

> *C = Challenge yourself to new heights.*

Now D:

> *D = Develop determination.*

Let me define determination for you. It is the quality of being resolute and firm in purpose, thought and action. It is having your mind made up after considerable thought, research and investigation. It is remaining solid even in the face of obstacles.

In other words, determination means you just do not quit. After you have made the commitment to overcome the challenges, determination is what sees you through.

Have you ever known a happy quitter? I haven't. I have known many different types of people in my life, but there are a few types of people I have never met.

• I have never met a successful quitter.

• I have never met a quitter who deserved great respect.

• I have never met a quitter who ended up a winner.

Do you know the difference between a winner and a loser? A winner gets up again. He or she is left standing when others have fallen down from the frustration, the troubles, obstacles, discouragement, resistance and trials on the road to success and happiness. A winner is the one who does not quit.

Following Christ is all about getting back up again. The Bible says, the righteous man may fall seven times but he gets back up again (Proverbs 24:16).

We need to be like the absent-minded professor in the old Disney movie who developed flubber, a substance that bounced back repeatedly without losing its energy. We need to coat ourselves in spiritual flubber so that if we slip and fall, we bounce back higher than before. We need to defy gravity with our faith.

What is the secret ingredient of spiritual flubber? Determination, and you can have some.

> Therefore, since we are surrounded by such a great cloud of witnesses, let us throw off everything that hinders and the sin that so easily entangles, and let us run with perseverance the race marked out for us.
>
> — Hebrews 12:1

• *Bounce-back Principle Number One: You will face obstacles and trials.*

Everyone in Heaven today faced trials while on earth, and so will you. Jesus said:

> ...If they persecuted me, they will persecute you also...
>
> — John 15:20b

> Let us fix our eyes on Jesus, the author and perfecter of our faith, who for the joy set before him endured the cross, scorning its shame, and sat down at the right hand of the throne of God.
>
> — Hebrews 12:2

Want to hear a surprise statement? Jesus did not want to go to the cross, and even prayed that God the Father would spare Him that ugly death. But it was not possible. Jesus went to the cross not with desire, but with determination. He knew it was necessary if we were going to get into the kingdom and live forever with Him. He had to go to the cross to die for the sin of the world. It was His heavenly mandate.

If that is what Jesus, the very Son of God, went through, do we expect our own lives to be cupcakes and roses all the time? Of course, none of us has to hang on the cross — that has been done, hallelujah! But we will have to develop the same determination that took Jesus to the cross if we are to succeed.

In your struggle against sin, you have not yet resisted to the point of shedding your blood.

— Hebrews 12:4

We sing that old hymn, "I have decided to follow Jesus," but maybe the words should be changed to, "I am determined to follow Jesus." There is a big difference. People make decisions all the time. At my church we have had services in which hundreds of people came forward and made decisions for Christ. Out of that number, maybe only thirty percent made a *determination* to go all the way. Only a handful seized the promise of God and saw it through with patience, perseverance and determination.

There can be discouragements in life. There are obstacles. There are roadblocks — expect it. When God promised the Israelites the promised land, He did not promise them an easy ride. There were still enemies in the promised land who had to be driven out. Many people think when they come to Christ, it is going to be sweet music until the hereafter, but that is wishful thinking. There are trials that require determination.

Finishing Strong

Any worthwhile dream or venture will face difficulties, resistance, setbacks, misunderstandings, struggles, opposition and problems. Those who have not accepted responsibility for their own life, who have not dreamed big dreams, who have not challenged themselves to reach higher and made the determination to go through with Jesus are going to be bumped to the side of the road.

You see it happen all the time. The highways and byways of life are lined with people who have gone off the road, blown a tire, rolled the car and are laying in the median wondering what happened. Instead of getting back in the race, they decide to camp out where no progress is being made.

Solomon wrote that finishing a thing is better than starting a thing.

Finishing is better than starting!

— Ecclesiastes 7:8a (TLB)

How many times have you started a book and read half way through, then found it a year later with your bookmark still in the middle?

How many have started knitting that blanket for a new nephew, then set it aside and felt guilty about it for years?

Perseverance matters not just in books and blankets, but in our fruitfulness in the Kingdom. Jesus told about the sower who threw seed out, some of it falling on good ground, some among the thorns, some on rocks and some by the wayside. The seed by the wayside did not have any roots, so when persecution came, it withered up. Some fell on rocks and they, too, failed to produce. Those among thorns desired riches and pleasure, and the life was choked out of them.

But Matthew 13:8 says:

Still other seed fell on good soil, where it produced a crop — a hundred, sixty or thirty times what was sown.

And Luke 8:15 says:

> But the seed on good soil stands for those with a noble and good heart, who hear the word, retain it, and by persevering produce a crop.

Do you want to be a 30-, 60-, 100-fold type of person? The word Jesus used, "perseverance," is a synonym for determination. It means we covered ourselves with "spiritual flubber" and bounced back every time somebody or something tried to steal our promises.

I am a big fan of the bounce-back principle. Don't ever stop coming back to the throne of God. Every morning I say, "I am back again, Lord." I never hear him say, "Oh, no, not you again." No! He says to us, "Son, I am glad you're here. Daughter, nice to see you today. Let's chat about a few things."

Even when I mess up, or do not preach as well as I should, or do not win as many souls as I think I should, and feel like a jerk, a failure and a worm, God says, "Get over it. Get some more of that flubber on you and try again." God teaches me to bounce back. He is the God of another chance. With Him, it is not three strikes and you're out. There is no need to be embarrassed at coming back and trying again because that is what He wants. Children who bounce back. Children who are determined.

Small Beginnings

The first time I tried to preach, I fell off the platform. I told my wife I was not going to preach again as long as I lived. Then our pastor asked me to preach and she said, "You are not turning him down — you're going to preach." So I did, and everybody kept laughing at me. I finally stopped in the middle of my sermon and asked the congregation, "What is so funny?" I was nervous and hurt. I went home and told Mary Jo I was never going to preach again. She pointed her finger at me and said, "You are not a quitter. You are going to keep going back until you get it right."

Well, I still haven't got it right, but I keep coming back. I have this "spiritual flubber" on. If I had quit every time I was tempted to be discouraged, I would have been gone a long time ago. But I am the "flubber man." Every Sunday, I am back, trying harder, persevering, staying on the highway.

One time a church board from a large church in another city was visiting my church on a Sunday morning. They had lost their pastor and wanted to offer me the position. They came without telling me, wanting to check the place out on Sunday. I discovered later that they were prepared to make me an enticing offer. It just so happened that in that morning's message I was making a positive, encouraging point about perseverance and longevity, and to make that point, I said something to the effect of, "I want you all to know, if you want to get rid of me, forget it. I am a permanent fixture here. I am not leaving this church." It was intended to show my congregation my dedication to the Gospel and to the church I loved. I can only imagine how astonished those board members were to hear their candidate pledge allegiance to his home pulpit!

In 1961, nineteen-year-old Bruce Olson read an article about the Motilone Indians in Venezuela, a cruel people who killed missionaries who came to them. When an oil company came into their territory, they killed sixty-three oil workers, and the government of Venezuela decided they would wipe out the entire Motilone Indian tribe because they were so violent.

Olson started having compassion for the Motilones. He could not get the support of his church, and his parents did not want him to go, but he felt God had called him to reach the Motilones. He bought a one-way ticket to Venezuela, took only a backpack, and said, "If I die, I die. But God has put a love in my heart for a people I have never met."

He went into the mountains where the Motilone Indians lived. As he hiked, he felt something sharp pierce his leg. He had been struck by an arrow. Suddenly, he was surrounded by Motilone Indians poking at him, cutting his skin. They imprisoned him and started talking about what they were going to do. He realized he had gotten dysentery and knew if he did not get help soon, he would die. He had to escape, but nobody had ever escaped from the Motilones. Somehow, that night, by a miracle of God, he escaped and made it to medical help.

A few weeks later, Olson put his backpack on and went back up to the Motilone tribe. He was captured, imprisoned and escaped again. Now the Motilones thought he must be a god. Nobody has ever escaped from them before. He had developed hepatitis, sought treatment, and came back a few months later. This time, they did not capture him but said, "What is with you? This is the third time you have come up here. Are you a god or something?" He said, "I am not, but there is a God in Heaven that you cannot see who sent His Son to die on a cross for you." He went through the whole Gospel, and those Motilones fell on their knees and received Jesus Christ. The whole tribe converted and became some of the most gentle people on the planet.

Why? The grace of God, of course. But also because one man was determined to follow the dream, the call of God on his life. He was not going to let hepatitis, dysentery, captivity or even a sword stop him. He was determined, and that is what brought him success. Determined people are successful people.

God's Will Revealed

Many people go to prayer without determination saying, "God, I pray that You will do this, if it be Thy will. Bless me, if it be Thy will. Heal me, if it be Thy will. Save my son, if it be Thy will."

I cannot stand that kind of praying, and I am pretty sure God can't either. He has made vast portions of His will known to us. He has given us plenty of knowledge to pray in faith for things we are certain He wants. Lazy people pray, "If it be thy will." The only time we really need to pray that way is when we are absolutely in the dark, confused about the situation and do not know God's perfect will. But in all other circumstances we pray what we know His will to be already.

He WANTS to bless.

He WANTS to heal.

He WANTS to prosper us.

He WANTS to save the lost.

I recently received a letter from a lady who wrote, "Pray that I will be able to tithe." I am not going to pray that because tithing is a decision. Anyone with any amount of money can do it. There are certain things I will not pray with people about because they already know the will of God. Why should I waste prayers when these sluggards lack determination to follow even the simplest commands? Lazy people obscure the will of God, or make it out to be more mysterious than it is. Determination takes hold of the blessings and benefits we know God has already promised. When we pray for those things we can say, "Lord, it is thy will, so let it be done!"

Jacob the patriarch did not play games with God. He got hold of God and said, "I am not going to let you go until you bless me." Imagine talking to God like that! What did God do? He blessed him! God loves determined people. God loves to bless people who are persistent, tenacious; people who hang in there. (See Genesis 32.)

Even the world respects determined people. Do you want people to think you are a genius? You may be less talented, less educated and less brilliant than the average person, but you can be considered a genius if you do just one thing: Stick to something long enough. It does not mean you are better than anybody else. It just shows you have staying power.

Determination will elevate you in the eyes of men, and of God.

• *Bounce-back Principle Number Two: Hell cannot stop you.*

When you are determined to do something that you know is God's will, none of hell's forces can stop you from achieving it. There is no devil on earth who can muster the strength to stop you.

I know of a man who burnt his legs seriously as a young man. Doctors said they had to amputate them, but he and his parents refused the operation and said they were going to believe God for a miracle. A few days went by and the doctors said, "I guess you were right. We do not have to amputate them. But you will never walk again, young man." The young man replied, "I will walk again," and when they wheeled him out of that hospital several months later, he went to his house and began walking a path along the picket fence in the yard, taking one step at a time and using the fence for support. He did not always feel like getting out there and walking, but he knew he had to if he was going to walk again.

Today, that young man, Glen Cunningham, is known as one of the greatest marathon runners in all of history.

What if he would have quit? What if he would have given up? People quit too soon, sometimes just before the miracle arrives. In 1915, the British Army was attacking the Turks. A terrific barrage of gunfire came from the shore and three British ships were lost. At noon, the British Navy decided to pull out, but what they did not know was this — the Turks had only sixty seconds of ammunition left. If the British had stayed one minute longer, they would have broken up the enemy forces; the war would have ended years before it did and millions of lives would have been spared. But they quit sixty seconds too soon.

How many people quit sixty seconds before their miracle arrives? How many people stop three feet short of their destiny? There was a man in the 1960s who sold everything to buy a piece of property in Texas because he knew there was oil on it. He started drilling for oil, but did not find it immediately. Then he thought he had better sell out before he lost everything, so he sold the land to an oil company who came in and drilled three feet deeper and struck one of the biggest veins of oil in Texas history. The man would have been a billionaire, but he stopped three feet short.

How many people quit three feet short? How many people stop the attack on the devil sixty seconds before victory?

What if the Wright brothers, these two Methodist boys, had decided it was true? Man cannot fly. Gravity cannot be defied. What if Orville and Wilbur had listened to the naysayers of the day? After all, Sir Isaac Newton taught us the law of gravity, and we all know that you cannot oppose the law of gravity. The odds were against these two. Even their father, a Methodist preacher, said, "If God meant for man to fly he would have given him wings."

But they believed something else. They believed that verse that says:

> ...all things are possible to him that believeth.
>
> — Mark 9:23b (KJV)

They believed it was possible to mount up with wings as eagles, to see as the birds see, and they kept at it until they had a successful lift off. In a short period of time, people were flying airplanes for all sorts of purposes, from battles to missions trips to vacations.

I remember meeting a ninety-year-old pilot who showed me his pilot certificate which had been signed by Wilbur Wright, who was in charge of what is now known as the Federal Aviation Administration. It was not that long ago that airplanes were invented, and in just a few generations' time, air travel has revolutionized the way we live.

• *Bounce-back Principle Number Three: When you are determined, there is great reward.*

Shammah was a private in David's army, in charge of defending a pea patch against the Philistines. One day, hundreds of Philistines came over the crest of the mountain, causing the other privates to flee. But Shammah stood there. "My job is to guard this pea patch. It does not matter if there are four hundred or four thousand Philistines. My job has not changed. I am determined to guard this pea patch and not let the enemy take even one pea."

Here came one Philistine and he whacked his head off. Another Philistine came by and shoved Shammah down, but he had his spiritual flubber on and popped back up. He whacked off the head of another Philistine, and another until he had single-handedly driven back hundreds of Philistines.

Shammah was promoted from a private to a general, from being an enlisted man to taking the highest official position in the king's army. He was made one of three senior leaders. He was honored; he was given great wealth and his fame spread throughout the whole nation. Why? Because he defended a pea patch. He would not let the enemy take even that. (See 2 Samuel 23.)

That is the kind of people God seems to work miracles through. He seems pleased with those who say, "This may be just a pea patch, but it is God's pea patch and nobody is going to get even a pea out of it while I am on duty." Great rewards lie waiting for people who are determined to valiantly defend what God has given them.

In Jesus' ministry we see it time and again. He never sent someone away who was determined. The woman with the issue of blood touched Him and was healed. Did she hang back and say, "I wonder if it is God's will for me to quit bleeding?" No! She pressed in. She was determined.

> And, behold, a woman, which was diseased with an issue of blood twelve years, came behind *him*, and touched the hem of his garment: For she said within herself, If I may but touch his garment, I shall be whole. But Jesus turned him about, and when he saw her, he said, Daughter, be of good comfort; thy faith hath made thee whole. And the woman was made whole from that hour.
>
> — Matthew 9:20-22 (KJV)

Another woman came to Jesus and said her daughter was possessed by a devil. Jesus turned and said, "It is not right to give bread to dogs." She could have said, "Boy, he offended me. I am going to quit following Him." But she was determined, and in the next few moments she received her miracle.

> Then Jesus went thence, and departed into the coasts of Tyre and Sidon. And, behold, a woman of Canaan came out of the same coasts, and cried unto him, saying, Have mercy on me, O Lord, *thou* Son of David; my daughter is grievously vexed with a devil. But he answered her not a word. And his disciples came and besought him, saying, Send her away; for she crieth after us. But he answered and said, I am not sent but unto the lost sheep of the house of Israel. Then came she and worshipped him, saying, Lord, help me. But he answered and said, It is not meet to take the children's bread, and to cast *it* to dogs. And she said, Truth, Lord: yet the dogs eat of the crumbs which fall from their masters' table. Then Jesus answered and said unto her, O woman, great *is* thy faith: be it unto thee even as thou wilt. And her daughter was made whole from that very hour.
>
> — Matthew 15:21-28 (KJV)

Jesus was determined. He knew what He was doing all the time, and kept His hand to the plow. One time Herod sent for Jesus because he wanted to see Him do a miracle. His servants came and said, "Jesus, King Herod wants to see you." Jesus said the most derogatory thing he ever said about anybody. He said:

> Go tell that fox, 'I will drive out demons and heal people today and tomorrow, and on the third day I will reach my goal.'
>
> — Luke 13:32

In other words, He did not have time for Herod's nonsense. Back then, "fox" was a slang word for homosexual.

You see, Jesus was determined. He was going to do what He had been called to do and not even the king was going to stop him.

God is looking for some determined people like that today. He is looking for people who are not just making decisions for Jesus, but making determinations for Jesus. He is looking for those who will choose total resolution and determination; those that will put their hand to the plow and go all the way through, not looking to the left or right, but going through as the Lord's anointed ones.

You can and will bounce back. Determination will take you through. Jesus' infusion of power will propel you toward His promises. The Bible says that we ought always to pray, not to faint. Not to quit. If you keep planting, in due season you will reap.

Whatever is meant for your harm, God will turn it for your good *if you do not give up*. No weapon formed against you will prosper, and the Lord will fight for you as you develop determination.

What obstacles do you face right now? What has your response been? How do you want to change your response? In what ways can you become more determined?

Power Point Questions:

☐ 1. When was the last time you had strong determination in the face of an adverse situation?

☐ 2. Rate your level of determination on a scale of one to ten.

☐ 3. What are you determined about right now?

Chapter Six

Good Exercise

Something has been happening to you as you have been reading this book. Maybe you have not noticed it; maybe you have.

Faith has been sneaking up on you. This book is full of Bible passages that bolster your faith, and by reading them, or hearing them, faith has begun to blossom in your heart.

You may think I am guessing at this, but I am not. I am simply believing what the Word says.

> So then faith *cometh* by hearing, and hearing by the word of God.
>
> — Romans 10:17 (KJV)

That is the next key:

E = EXERCISE faith.

It is the best kind of exercise you can do! Flabby faith is worthless faith. Without faith, it is impossible to please God. Without faith, our dreams are merely dreams. Without faith, we achieve nothing.

With faith, we have the springboard of success in life.

- We can blast away mountains.

- Promises become realities.

- The unseen becomes seen.

- Impossibilities become possibilities.

- The imagined becomes actual.

I was flying out of Portland, Oregon, and flew right over Mount Rainier, Mount Hood and Mount St. Helens. Those snow-covered peaks standing majestically along the mountain range reminded me of Jesus' teaching on faith:

> ...I tell you the truth, if you have faith as small as a mustard seed, you can say to this mountain, 'Move from here to there' and it will move. Nothing will be impossible for you.
>
> — Matthew 17:20

Most of us remember the eruption of Mount St. Helens in the early 1980s, which caused half of the dome to actually be removed in a matter of seconds.

But until the volcano blew, the mountain did not budge. In fact, there are dormant volcanoes all over the world that offer no threat because all they do is gurgle and steam, never living up to their threats.

It is not enough to have faith; we have to exercise it. James 2:17 and 26 says that faith without a corresponding action is dead. We cannot claim to have faith if our actions never show it.

> So also faith, if it does not have works (deeds and actions of obedience to back it up), by itself is destitute of power (inoperative, dead).
>
> — James 2:17 (AMP)

> For as the human body apart from the spirit is lifeless, so faith apart from [its] works of obedience is also dead.
>
> — James 2:26 (AMP)

All the treasures of Heaven await our release of faith. It is the substance that enables us to apprehend what already exists in the spiritual realm. In Matthew 21:18, Jesus gave the disciples a lesson in faith. Jesus did not curse too much, but in this case He did. He cursed a tree.

> Early in the morning, as he was on his way back to the city, he was hungry. Seeing a fig tree by the road, he went up to it but found nothing on it except leaves. Then he said to it, "May you never bear fruit again!" Immediately the tree withered.
>
> — Matthew 21:18-19

Jesus did not curse it because the tree made him angry, like some people do when cars cut in front of them, or shopping carts bump into their car door at the grocery store. He was getting ready to give the disciples a lesson in faith. Another Gospel account tells us it was a few days later that they actually noticed the withering of the tree, but the moment Jesus spoke those words of faith, the roots of that tree began to wither and die. When the disciples saw it, they marveled. Jesus told them:

> "I assure you, even if you had faith as small as a mustard seed you could say to this mountain, 'Move from here to there,' and it would move. Nothing would be impossible."
>
> — Matthew 17:20 (NLT)

That takes us to these two power principles in this faith lesson.

• *Number One: If you have faith and doubt not, you shall move the mountain.*

• *Number Two: We have to speak to the mountain to get a reaction.*

Usually when we face a struggle, we share our prayer requests at church or in Bible studies. "Please pray about the mountain I am facing." But did you notice Jesus did not say anything about praying in the first part of his lesson? He said, "*Say* to this mountain."

Say!

When we face a mountain, a problem, a struggle, it is time to speak *to it* instead of speaking *about it* to everybody else.

You see, faith can call things that are not as though they are.

> ...God, who quickeneth the dead, and calleth those things which be not as though they were.
>
> — Romans 4:17c (KJV)

Jesus looked at that unproductive fig tree and said it would not bear anymore fruit, and it withered up. Yes, maybe you are facing a mountain. Maybe you are facing a big obstacle in your life. Jesus said you can speak to it and tear it down, by faith. You have the authority to call those things which are not as though they are. You may still see it with your eyes, but what we see with our natural senses is not as important as what we see in the Spirit.

Faith And Hope

> So we fix our eyes not on what is seen, but on what is unseen. For what is seen is temporary, but what is unseen is eternal.
>
> — 2 Corinthians 4:18

Hebrews says faith is the substance of things hoped for (11:1). That means it is the substantiation of our dream. You can see a promise in God's Word and say, "I hope that comes to pass," but hoping is not going to move the hand of God. Hope describes the picture; faith paints the canvas. I might tell someone on my staff to paint a patriotic mural on our wall for a fourth of July celebration, and I would describe the colors and the people I want depicted. I might even sketch it on a piece of paper. That is all vision-building — hope. But until they take paint, get the paintbrush, and start painting, there will be no mural on the wall. Faith carries out the vision.

Acts 14:8 begins the account of Paul and his evangelistic team coming through Lystra.

> In Lystra there sat a man crippled in his feet, who was lame from birth and had never walked.

This man had never known the joy of walking to school, or church, or hiking through a forest. But now he heard Paul — really heard him — and faith came to him:

> He listened to Paul as he was speaking. Paul looked directly at him, saw that he had faith to be healed.
>
> — Acts 14:9

Paul did not perceive that the man had been hoping and praying to be healed. It does not say that the man was kind enough to be healed, or filled with enough love to be healed, or lived a good life and deserved to be healed, though all of those things may have been true. Paul saw that he had **faith** to be healed.

Many people say, "I am hoping and praying that my whole family will get saved." Go ahead and hope and pray, but add to it *speaking* and *acting*. Add substance to your hope. Begin to speak to the mountain, not *about* it.

Are you talking about the mountain, or to it? I remember the healing evangelists in the 1950s who had such success. Thousands of people were healed, but you never heard the evangelists pray for the sick. They made faith commands. "Get up out of the wheelchair!" "Thou spirit of disease, I command you to come out in the name of Jesus!"

Speaking faith and acting on faith is exercising faith. You might say, "I cannot speak a lie. The doctor told me there is no cure." Here is the test for knowing whether you are speaking lies or speaking faith. Is what you are saying in harmony with God's Word? If it is, you are speaking by faith. I don't care what the doctor or accountant or lawyer's report is, the real report is found in the pages from Genesis through Revelation. It is your choice which you will believe.

Paul chose to believe what he saw in the Spirit rather than what he saw in the natural. He spoke with a loud voice to the man's mountain, his crippledness, and his words ushered in a new reality, verse ten:

...Stand upright on thy feet...

— Acts 14:10b (KJV)

What did the man do? "Paul, you do not understand. I do not know how to stand up. I have never done it before. They told me at the hospital that I would never walk." No, this man had the faith to be healed, and when Paul spoke the word of faith, the man acted instantly. I can hear the snap, crackle and pop of those skinny legs as they took their new assignment.

The Demonstration

One problem with evangelical Christianity as a whole is that we know a lot of doctrine and theology, but we rarely experience a demonstration of the Gospel. Doctrine and theology must be experienced to be truly life-changing; head knowledge alone is useless, and can even get in the way of a demonstration of divine power.

I have heard stories about evangelical missions organizations who sent missionaries to places like Africa. They were there building roads, wells, hospitals and schools — but so were secular organizations, and nobody was really being affected by the Gospel. The Christians had no power.

One missionary, now a professor at a highly respected Christian university, was troubled by this, and attributed it to the fact that the missionaries knew how to talk about casting devils, but never cast out devils. They talked about healing the sick, but never saw the sick healed. The people still went to witch doctors after attending Gospel crusades because the witch doctors seemed to have more spiritual power.

The missionaries were not allowing the power of faith to overwhelm the dark powers that were at work through ungodly pagan religions.

That particular missionary, and many others, reversed course and began to educate themselves in spiritual matters. Soon, they were doing hand-to-hand combat with the forces of darkness, and winning. They began to lay hands on the sick and cast out devils, and people started coming to Christ by the thousands.

You see, it is not just by speaking enticing words of man's wisdom, but by demonstrating God's power that we gain victory.

And my speech and my preaching *were* not with persuasive words of human wisdom, but in

> demonstration of the Spirit and of power, that
> your faith should not be in the wisdom of men,
> but in the power of God.
>
> — 1 Corinthians 2:4-5 (NKJV)

Do you want power in your life? Speak God's
Word. Take it seriously. Quit hoping for something
to change, and start employing faith. The man Paul
healed did not just hope to be healed; he added faith
to that hope. Faith meant believing — and doing.
Faith is not a mental exercise alone. People say, "I
am standing on the Word." What do they mean? Too
often it means they are believing but not acting, like
a soldier hunkered down in a foxhole but refusing to
fire a shot. Be like the missionaries. If you have a lack
of power, ask yourself why, and then go after it. Begin speaking *to* your problems like Jesus, Paul and
the disciples did.

What Faith Did For Abraham

Abraham exercised faith, and we are the rightful
inheritors of his legacy. Romans chapter four says that
you and I are children of Abraham.

> Therefore, the promise comes by faith, so that it
> may be by grace and may be guaranteed to all
> Abraham's offspring — not only to those who
> are of the law but also to those who are of the
> faith of Abraham. He is the father of us all.
>
> — Romans 4:16

Paul reaffirmed this in Galatians that Christians, if we have faith, are children of Abraham. In other words, all the promises and blessings God gave to Abraham belong to us — **if** we have faith.

The Bible says Abraham was counted righteous because of faith. Today you and I are counted righteous because of faith, even if you do not feel very righteous. It does not matter what you feel. Faith says, "I am the righteousness of God in Christ because of what Jesus did for me on the cross, even when I am acting like a jerk!"

I used to live a life that was up and down. Every time I had a bad thought, I thought I had fallen out of good standing with God. Every time I said a wrong word, or lost my temper, or did something bad, I thought I had lost my position as a believer. Then I learned that because of my faith in Jesus Christ, I am never in bad standing with God. I am always in a place of righteousness because I am in Christ and Christ is in me.

I used to think I had to respond to altar calls every Sunday because I had messed up during the week. I remember losing my temper with somebody one day and throwing a milk carton at him. This was a long time ago. Now I find that as I abide in Jesus, and abide in His words, sanctification begins to take place. It is not an overnight phenomenon. I found that my relationship with God is now steady, no longer tenuous, no longer depending on me. It depends on my faith in what Jesus did for me already.

What a great place to live! And it is all because we, like Abraham, have been counted righteous because of our faith.

Faith also brought Abraham great wealth, another blessing of God. Many Christians have been taught that wealth is a curse that leads to greed and covetousness. In truth, I know poor people who are more greedy and covetous than some of the rich people I know. I cannot say that I see differing levels of greed in people with different incomes. It is not a matter of money or wealth, but a matter of the heart. A person living in poverty and dreaming of money and buying lottery tickets can be greedier than a millionaire.

Abraham was a tither. He honored God with his wealth. I was in South Africa and preached to eight thousand people in a huge church made up of many poor people. The pastor announced he was going to take an offering for me, and I said, "No, no, brother. I did not come for an offering." He said to me, "These are poor people. The only way to get them out of poverty is to teach them to give." That pastor was wisely leading his people to act on faith to get them out of their situation.

Many preachers say that faith is exemplified by poverty, because that is when Christians depend on God for everything. Some Christians see a nobility in poverty, as if material lack automatically means inner spiritual wealth. They will misquote passages from the Bible that are supposed to make wealth seem worldly, corrupting and indicative of bad character. Why, then, did God make the father of faith wealthy? Yes, money can be worldly, corrupting and breed bad character, but wealth for the believer is a blessing from God, an answer to our faith and a tool for His Kingdom.

Faith also brought Abraham special guidance from God. He was called a friend of God. When God wanted to do something on earth, He came down and talked to Abraham about it first, as in the case of Sodom and Gomorrah. Likewise, Jesus said:

> I no longer call you servants, because a servant does not know his master's business. Instead, I have called you friends, for everything that I learned from my Father I have made known to you.
>
> — John 15:15

That is a benefit of faith. You can be the kind of person God speaks to about His plans, not just the one who carries them out. Before He does something in your city, He comes over to your house and sits down at your kitchen table and talks it over with you, not because you are in charge, but because you are His friend.

Can you imagine having that kind of friendship with God? Faith makes it possible.

Let me recap three steps for putting faith into action:

• *1. Decide whether what you are believing for, lines up with the Bible.* Faith must be rooted in a promise of God, not in our own cleverness or ideas. His promises are so good we do not need to dream anything else up.

• *2. Speak the promise and not the problem.* Speak to the mountain, not about it.

• *3. Take action based on faith, not based on sight or sound.* Trust your spiritual sense more than your physical senses.

Power Point Questions:

☐ 1. What circumstance in your life requires you to exercise faith?

☐ 2. What was your greatest test of faith?

☐ 3. How do you exercise faith in practical ways?

Chapter Seven

Forgetting The Past

I was driving one day and passed a car that had pulled off the side of the road. As I passed by, I looked in the rear view mirror to see if everything was okay. All of a sudden I felt a bump and I realized I had hit the car in front of me.

I had ignored my own advice to new converts, which is, "You cannot go very far in your Christian life if you keep staring in the rear view mirror."

That brings us to our sixth principle:

F = FORGET The Past.

Life was not meant to be lived in the rear view mirror. The past can teach us lessons, but we cannot live there. If we do, we open the door to failure and unhappiness.

I believe there is a curse associated with trying to live in the past. As we pass through time in these capsules we call bodies, we are literally trapped in the present. We cannot change the past, or live there again, and we cannot single-handedly determine the future. To try to live in the past is a curse. To try to live in the future is a curse. We can glance in the rear view mirror now and then and thank God we are not back there anymore, but what a mistake to stare into it while trying to move ahead.

There is a terrific text from the Bible that speaks on this issue. In Philippians chapter three, Paul wrote about his past as a Pharisee, his education, and everything he did that he once thought was good.

> **But whatever was to my profit I now consider loss for the sake of Christ.**
>
> — **Philippians 3:7**

He went on to say that he viewed his whole past as dung, or manure, compared to the excellency of knowing Christ.

That is a pretty strong statement about his past! Do you consider everything that came before your salvation like that? Is your past as valuable to you as a manure heap compared to what you have now in your knowledge of Christ?

The "Good ol' Days?"

Paul, who had known the Lord thirty years by this time, said in Philippians 3:12, that he had not yet attained nor become perfect, but was still trying to apprehend that for which Christ had apprehended him. He said, "But one thing I do," and then he listed two things that really comprise two sides of the same thought.

> ...forgetting what is behind and straining toward what is ahead, I press on toward the goal to win the prize for which God has called me heavenward in Christ Jesus.
>
> — Philippians 3:13a-14

Paul did not believe in the good ol' days, and he did not try to reside there. There is nothing more damaging than to hear a pastor get up and say, "Christians are not what they used to be. Why, back in the old days we would have prayer meetings all night long. The kids would be there and then we would go out and plow the fields in the morning. We would not even be tired." They try to make you feel like you are half a Christian because you went to one prayer meeting this month and it lasted forty minutes. We forget that those all-night prayer meetings were not held every week or even every month, and we forget about all the problems (financial and otherwise), churches had back then. Those were not really the good ol' days. The good ol' days are here and now, just as the Holy Spirit is the Spirit of the now.

The children of Israel tried to live in the past, and it angered God. They were slaves in the land of Egypt, eating the leftovers, the garbage, working from morning until night without the necessary tools, whipped, beaten and mistreated. God raised up Moses to lead them out of their bondage, then provided food for them in the form of highly nutritious manna, full of everything a person needs to keep healthy. And what did they say? "We sure had it better when we were back in Egypt. Remember the food? Those were the good ol' days."

Thinking like that brought a curse on them. Many of them died from snake bites and sickness. Their minds had rewritten history so that God appeared to be the bad guy, not the good guy.

You and I do that, too. Past hurts can seem bigger than they really were. Past successes can seem that way, too. Every once in awhile, you may hear an old song that takes you right back to high school or childhood. When I was in school, everybody wore English Leather or Jade East colognes. They are not as popular now, but sometimes I catch a whiff of English Leather or Jade East in an airport and have a flash-back. It is amazing how the senses can try to steer our minds and make us do u-turns in life.

Jesus said:

> "No one who puts his hand to the plow and looks back is fit for service in the kingdom of God."

— Luke 9:62

People who want to fixate on something in the past and dwell on it, bemoan it, regret it, or celebrate it, tend to never succeed in the now.

I know a man who was running a shady business before the federal government shut him down. For years after that, all he could talk about was how the government did him wrong. Within seven years, this man, who was not old, developed a disease where he shook and could not control himself. He could not even walk. And still, every time you would meet the man, he would tell you what happened years ago, and how the government shut his business down and destroyed his life.

He let the past destroy him. The past cannot destroy you unless you let it. Jesus came to wipe out that man's past, and yours and mine. The past sins, the past evil, and even the past successes are wiped out and become nothing to us, compared to knowing Christ.

Forgiving Others — And Yourself

Maybe you were a victim in the past. Statistics tell me that many of the people I meet every day, whether I know it or not, have been rejected, hurt, mistreated or abused somehow. The pain is often so bad they can barely stand it, and the memories keep coming back.

Jesus knows your hurt. He knows what happened in your past and understands because He was abused, mistreated, rejected, betrayed and abandoned. He was put on a cross, hung there and died. And yet He said:

> ...Behold, I make all things new...
>
> — **Revelation 21:5b (KJV)**

He can take your hurt and turn it around. He can take your mistakes and turn them into miracles, but you have to let him.

How do we forget the past? Paul tells us we can do it by moving steadily toward the future, refusing to dwell on thoughts about our past hurts.

Doris Wagner, wife of author and professor Peter Wagner, is an expert in getting people delivered from demonic oppression and possession. She says one of the key entry points that demons have into a person's life is unforgiveness. She explains scripturally how unforgiveness is the devil's snare, and how people tend to live there and feel that their whole life is affected because of what happened. They do not understand that there is an emissary of Satan manipulating their life. While their spirit may not be possessed, it seems that this evil entity is controlling their thoughts and actions, and they cannot seem to break loose.

No matter what your past is, you can become a great hero in God's Kingdom if you will live in the now and press toward the future. Peter failed the Lord miserably, but bounced back. Judas failed the Lord, could not get over it and committed suicide. The first sermon Peter preached after denying the Lord Jesus Christ won more than three thousand people to Christ. Peter got on with his life! He could not change his mistake, but he could repent and press on.

Out Of Gangs

I met the late Tom Skinner years ago when I was a regent at a Christian university. Tom Skinner was a pillar and a prophet in the evangelical community, particularly among African Americans. As a young man he led a Harlem gang and rejected the Christianity of his parents, figuring his fate was going to be the same as many of his friends who died on the streets.

One day, Tom was listening to the radio and heard an unpolished preacher say that in Christ old things pass away and we become new creations. Tom sensed that Jesus really could take the mistakes of the past and turn them into miracles, and so he prayed that Jesus would come into his life and change him from a Harlem gang leader into a man of God.

Tom Skinner went on to become one of the greatest preachers and leaders of our time, motivating tens of thousands of people, telling them that their past does not have to determine their future, getting them out of situations they thought they would live in forever. I remember when we asked him to address the student body at the university, he stood at that podium, and with such eloquence, motivated those students to reach their greatest potential in Christ regardless of their past. I sat there with warmth going through my very being as he said that God really does take our past, especially our sins, and casts them in the deepest sea, taking them as far as the east is from the west.

> "Forget the former things; do not dwell on the past. See, I am doing a new thing! Now it springs up; do you not perceive it?..."
>
> — Isaiah 43:18-19a
>
> I will repay you for the years the locust have eaten...
>
> — Joel 2:25a

> For I will forgive their wickedness and remember their sins no more.

> — Hebrews 8:12

Yesterday is gone and tomorrow is a clean slate. Longtime Miami Dolphins head coach Don Shula was the coach with the most wins in the history of the National Football League, and he had a twenty-four-hour rule I think everyone should adopt. He allowed himself and his players a maximum of twenty-four hours after a football game to either celebrate the victory or bemoan the defeat. Once the twenty-four hours ended, they could not talk about it anymore. All they could do was focus their energies on preparing for the next opponent.

That is what Paul was saying, forgetting those things which are behind, and reaching ahead to those things which are before, and in so doing we press toward the mark of the prize of the high calling in Christ Jesus. Failure is never fatal when you turn your mistakes over to Jesus.

A New View

God can reframe your past, giving you a different picture of what happened and what it meant. Back in 1992, a journalist asked wealthy presidential candidate Ross Perot, "Is it true you are trying to buy the White House?" Perot knew it was true, so he replied, "Yes! I am trying to buy it for the people because they cannot afford it for themselves because the politicians made it too expensive." He turned it around so that what was meant as negative now appeared positive.

God does that with our lives. When the devil throws an accusation at us based on past sin or mistakes, God whips it around and makes it positive.

My good friend, Richard Dortch, was the president of the PTL television network before he lost everything in the wake of that scandal. A year before the PTL blow-up, a pastor and renowned prophet called Richard Dortch and said, "I have a Word from the Lord for you. God is going to shut down PTL because of the sins there." Dortch said, "What am I supposed to do?" And the prophet answered, "Correct it. Get rid of those who are sinning because they are bringing a curse on the whole ministry. Call the people to repentance."

Dortch took the prophet seriously and invited him to PTL, but the prophet would not come. So Dortch had a staff meeting and said, "I received a call from a man we all know and respect, and he said God is going to shut PTL down in one year if we do not repent. The people who give to PTL have the right to know that the people who run PTL are living holy lives." He named off every sin that the prophet had exposed to him.

The staff shrugged him off, and within one year PTL was shut down. People tried to keep it alive, but they couldn't. For two years, Dortch would pick up the paper and find his picture there, along with Jim Bakker's. Soon he was indicted. All of his money, everything that he had in retirement and annuities, had to be cashed in to pay for lawyers to defend him. Because he could not stop the things that he knew were going on, the judge ordered him to spend sixteen years in a federal penitentiary.

Dortch served eighteen months of the sentence, and because of all the stress had to have several surgeries right in prison. He lost a kidney to cancer and was forced to walk with an aluminum walker for six months. He was once a celebrated individual, a hero of young pastors all across America, and was now in federal prison because he covered up, rather than exposed wrong doing. He lost his credentials, and none of his friends wanted to talk to him. As the Bible says:

> **He who conceals his sins does not prosper, but whoever confesses and renounces them finds mercy.**
>
> **— Proverbs 28:13**

One day a letter came to Dortch while he was in prison. In the left-hand corner of the envelope was the name of the prophet who had prophesied PTL's downfall. Dortch's heart fell. What else could go wrong? The last thing he wanted were more prophecies about his life. He had already lost it all. While other prisoners were going to their meal, Richard went to his cell and wept, afraid to open the envelope. He prayed. "God I have failed you. I have failed everybody who has ever known me and trusted me, and if there is more hard news that I need, give me the grace to receive it."

When he opened the letter, the first words he read were these: "Brother Dortch, I love you. I have a Word from the Lord. God will restore all the years the cankerworm has eaten. When you are released, He is going to give you such an abounding harvest that all shall be made up to you. It will be as if nothing has been lost. You need not make up anything for Him; He will make it up to you."

What a tender loving Father we serve! Dortch was released from prison. His first ministry opportunity was at Calvary Temple in Dallas, under pastor J. Don George. Dortch walked into the pulpit afraid, embarrassed and said, "I need to ask you to forgive me for the shame I have brought to the Body of Christ." People's eyes opened, their mouths dropped. People started weeping throughout the congregation. Pastor George walked up, put his arm around Richard and said, "Richard, you never again need to address this congregation and ask forgiveness because you are forgiven."

Over the years, God has restored everything that was taken from Richard Dortch, just as He said He would. Dortch's integrity is back. He even went to visit the judge who sentenced him and gave him a big hug. He has written more books now than he ever did before he went to prison. His ministry is wider, he is helping more people, he regained his credentials and is an ordained minister of the Gospel once again. Everything he lost God restored to him — and a whole lot more.

It's true! You can lose it all and find it again if you will forget the past.

When old things pass away, keep them in the "old things" cemetery. Do not raise them up. Forget the past, give Jesus first place in your life, and you will remain on the highway to happiness and success.

Power Point Questions:

☐ 1. Do you need to forgive someone?

☐ 2. Do you need to forgive yourself for something you did?

☐ 3. What in your past do you need to forget, including the good things?

The Last Word

Together we have gone through six keys to success and happiness.

A = Accept responsibility for your own success and happiness

B = Be a big dreamer

C = Challenge yourself to new heights

D = Develop determination

E = Exercise faith

F = Forget the past

There are many, many more keys that will help us reach our destinies, but these form the basics, and if you put them into practice I guarantee you will get results now and for the rest of your life.

God wants you to be blessed, happy, healthy and prosperous. Your situation and your life are unique, but these principles are timeless. When you apply them to your life, they will be like a powerful chemical reaction that releases energy. God has built success into your life story, and these six elements, when mixed with your gifts and character, will prove unstoppable.

I look forward to hearing how your life has changed as a result of reading this book. Please write to me and add to my growing file of testimonies that show how God's principles work in regular, everyday life.

Now, let me add this prayer and in faith believe that these seeds will flourish.

> My dear friend, I pray for you now, in the Name of Jesus Christ!

> I pray that God will answer all your prayers when you call upon Him.

> I pray that the Lord will promote you to greater success and happiness and blessings than you have ever known before. I pray that He gives you advancement and increase, and that He sets you in a high place of influence and authority.

> I pray that God, the Father will . . .
> . . . support you,
> . . . refresh you,

... strengthen you,
... and grant you the desires of your heart.

I pray that the Lord will fulfill all your good plans, giving you His victory as you trust in His mercy, grace, strength, and favor.

May the Lord grant you an overflowing joy in everything you set your hand to do. May He not withhold even one request that comes from your lips.

I pray that God will enrich your life and send His personalized, invoked blessings upon your home, your work, your ministry, and your life.

May He grant you a long and fruitful life, filled with wonderful surprises from Heaven, giving you a life of splendor, majesty, integrity, and character that comes only through trusting His Son, Jesus Christ.

Yes, dear friend, I pray for you now, that God will make you a blessing to all who come into contact with you. And may He constantly assure you of His steadfast love for you forever.

I pray for you. I believe it and I decree it, by faith, for your life! In the Name of Jesus Christ. Amen.

To order this best-selling book by Pastor Dave Williams, mail this form with payment to:

THE HOPE STORE
202 South Creyts Road
Lansing, Michigan 48917-9284

or:

PHONE
517-321-2780
800-888-7284

FAX
517-321-6332

WRITE
202 S. Creyts Rd.
Lansing, MI 48917

Please enter my order as follows:

☐ NEW LIFE (English)
☐ LA NUEVA VIDA (Spanish)

2-25	_____	@1.95 ea.	_____
26-49	_____	@1.70 ea.	_____
50-99	_____	@1.50 ea.	_____
100-199	_____	@1.25 ea.	_____
200-349	_____	@1.10 ea.	_____
350-499	_____	@.95 ea.	_____
500+	_____	@.75 ea.	_____

Add 10% shipping/handling US _____
(15% shipping/handling Canada)
TOTAL INCLUDED WITH ORDER _____

Name _____

Business/Church _____

Address _____

City _____ State _____ ZIP _____

Telephone (_____) _____

Mastercard ☐   Visa ☐ (see below for ordering by credit card)

Authorized Signature _____

PLEASE SEND ME: One Case (150 books) of

☐ NEW LIFE (English)   ☐ LA NUEVA VIDA (Spanish)
at the SPECIAL price of $142.50 per box **US** and $169.50 **CAN**
(plus shipping — 10% US — 15% Canada)

MAIL ALL ORDERS TO: THE HOPE STORE
202 S. Creyts Rd. Lansing, MI 48917-9284

VISA/MASTERCARD ORDERS: Call 1-800-888-7284

About The Author

Dave Williams is pastor of Mount Hope Church and International Outreach Ministries, with world headquarters in Lansing, Michigan. He has served for over 20 years, leading the church in Lansing from 226 to over 4000 today. Dave sends trained ministers into unreached cities to establish disciple-making churches, and, as a result, today has "branch" churches in the United States, the Philippines, and in Africa.

Dave is the founder and president of Mount Hope Bible Training Institute, a fully accredited institute for training ministers and lay people for the work of the ministry. He has authored 45 books including the fifteen-time best seller, *The Start of Something Wonderful* (with over 2,000,000 books sold), and more recently, *The Miracle Results of Fasting,* and *The Road To Radical Riches.*

The Pacesetter's Path telecast is Dave's weekly television program seen over a syndicated network of secular stations, and nationally over the Sky Angel satellite system. Dave has produced over 125 audio cassette programs including the nationally acclaimed *School of Pacesetting Leadership* which is being used as a training program in churches around the United States, and in Bible schools in South Africa and the Philippines. He is a popular speaker at conferences, seminars, and conventions. His speaking ministry has taken him across America, Africa, Europe, Asia, and other parts of the world.

Along with his wife, Mary Jo, Dave established The Dave and Mary Jo Williams Charitable Mission (Strategic Global Mission), a mission's ministry for providing scholarships to pioneer pastors and grants to inner-city children's ministries.

Dave's articles and reviews have appeared in national magazines such as *Advance, The Pentecostal Evangel, Ministries Today, The Lansing Magazine, The Detroit Free Press* and others. Dave, as a private pilot, flies for fun. He is married, has two grown children, and lives in Delta Township, Michigan.

You may write to Pastor Dave Williams:

P.O. Box 80825

Lansing, MI 48908-0825

Please include your special prayer requests when you write, or you may call the Mount Hope Global Prayer Center anytime: (517) 327-PRAY

DECAPOLIS
PUBLISHING

For a catalog of products, call:

1-517-321-2780 or

1-800-888-7284

or visit us on the web at:

www.mounthopechurch.org

For Your Spiritual Growth

Here's the help you need for your spiritual journey. These books will encourage you, and give you guidance as you seek to draw close to Jesus and learn of Him. Prepare yourself for fantastic growth!

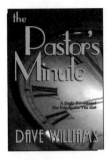

QUESTIONS I HAVE ANSWERED
Get answers to many of the questions you've always wanted to ask a pastor!

THE PASTOR'S MINUTE
A daily devotional for people on the go! Powerful topics will help you grow even when you're in a hurry.

ANGELS: THEY'RE WATCHING YOU!
The Bible tells more than you might think about these powerful beings.

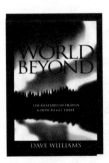

THE WORLD BEYOND
What will Heaven be like? What happens there? Will we see relatives who have gone before us? Who *REALLY* goes to Heaven?

FILLED!
Learn how you can be filled with the mightiest power in the universe. Find out what could be missing from your life.

STRATEGIC GLOBAL MISSION
Read touching stories about God's plan for accelerating the Gospel globally through reaching children and training pastors.

These and other books available from Dave Williams and:

DECAPOLIS PUBLISHING

For Your Spiritual Growth

Here's the help you need for your spiritual journey. These books will encourage you, and give you guidance as you seek to draw close to Jesus and learn of Him. Prepare yourself for fantastic growth!

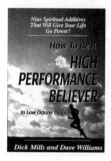

HOW TO BE A HIGH PERFORMANCE BELIEVER
Pour in the nine spiritual additives for real power in your Christian life.

SECRET OF POWER WITH GOD
Tap into the real power with God; the power of prayer. It will change your life!

THE NEW LIFE ...
You can get off to a great start on your exciting life with Jesus! Prepare for something wonderful.

MIRACLE RESULTS OF FASTING
You can receive MIRACLE benefits, spiritually and physically, with this practical Christian discipline.

WHAT TO DO IF YOU MISS THE RAPTURE
If you miss the Rapture, there may still be hope, but you need to follow these clear survival tactics.

THE AIDS PLAGUE
Is there hope? Yes, but only Jesus can bring a total and lasting cure to AIDS.

These and other books available from Dave Williams and:

DECAPOLIS PUBLISHING

For Your Spiritual Growth

Here's the help you need for your spiritual journey. These books will encourage you, and give you guidance as you seek to draw close to Jesus and learn of Him. Prepare yourself for fantastic growth!

THE ART OF PACESETTING LEADERSHIP
You can become a successful leader with this proven leadership development course.

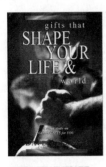

GIFTS THAT SHAPE YOUR LIFE
Learn which ministry best fits you, and discover your God-given personality gifts, as well as the gifts of others.

GROWING UP IN OUR FATHER'S FAMILY
You can have a family relationship with your heavenly father. Learn how God cares for you.

SUPERNATURAL SOULWINNING
How will we reach our family, friends, and neighbors in this short time before Christ's return?

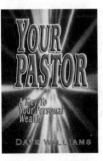

YOUR PASTOR: A KEY TO YOUR PERSONAL WEALTH
By honoring your pastor you can actually be setting yourself up for a financial blessing from God!

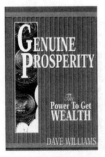

GENUINE PROSPERITY
Learn what it means to be truly prosperous! God gives us the power to get wealth!

These and other books available from Dave Williams and:

For Your Spiritual Growth

Here's the help you need for your spiritual journey. These books will encourage you, and give you guidance as you seek to draw close to Jesus and learn of Him. Prepare yourself for fantastic growth!

SOMEBODY OUT THERE NEEDS YOU
Along with the gift of salvation comes the great privilege of spreading the gospel of Jesus Christ.

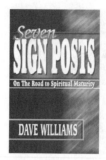

SEVEN SIGNPOSTS TO SPIRITUAL MATURITY
Examine your life to see where you are on the road to spiritual maturity.

THE PASTORS PAY
How much is your pastor worth? Who should set his pay? Discover the scriptural guidelines for paying your pastor.

DECEPTION, DELUSION & DESTRUCTION
Recognize spiritual deception and unmask spiritual blindness.

THE ROAD TO RADICAL RICHES
Are you ready to jump from "barely getting by" to Gods plan for putting you on the road to Radical Riches?

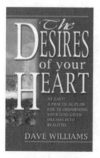

THE DESIRES OF YOUR HEART
Yes, Jesus wants to give you the desires of your heart, and make them realities.

These and other books available from Dave Williams and:

For Your Successful Life

These video cassettes will give you successful principles to apply to your whole life. Each a different topic, and each a fantastic teaching of how living by God's Word can give you total success!

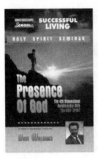

THE PRESENCE OF GOD
Find out how you can have a more dynamic relationship with the Holy Spirit.

FILLED WITH THE HOLY SPIRIT
You can rejoice and share with others in this wonderful experience of God.

GIFTS THAT CHANGE YOUR WORLD
Learn which ministry best fits you, and discover your God-given personality gifts, as well as the gifts of others.

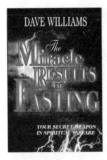

THE SCHOOL OF PACESETTING LEADERSHIP
Leaders are made, not born. You can become a successful leader with this proven leadership development course.

MIRACLE RESULTS OF FASTING
Fasting is your secret weapon in spiritual warfare. Learn how you'll benefit spiritually and physically! Six video messages.

A SPECIAL LADY
If you feel used and abused, this video will show you how you really are in the eyes of Jesus. You are special!

These and other videos available from Dave Williams and:

For Your Successful Life

These video cassettes will give you successful principles to apply to your whole life. Each a different topic, and each a fantastic teaching of how living by God's Word can give you total success!

HOW TO BE A HIGH PERFORMANCE BELIEVER
Pour in the nine spiritual additives for real power in your Christian life.

THE UGLY WORMS OF JUDGMENT
Recognizing the decay of judgment in your life is your first step back into God's fullness.

WHAT TO DO WHEN YOU FEEL WEAK AND DEFEATED
Learn about God's plan to bring you out of defeat and into His principles of victory!

WHY SOME ARE NOT HEALED
Discover the obstacles that hold people back from receiving their miracle and how God can help them receive the very best!

BREAKING THE POWER OF POVERTY
The principality of mammon will try to keep you in poverty. Put God FIRST and watch Him bring you into a wealthy place.

HERBS FOR HEALTH
A look at the concerns and fears of modern medicine. Learn the correct ways to open the doors to your healing.

These and other videos available from Dave Williams and:

DECAPOLIS PUBLISHING

Running Your Race

These simple but powerful audio cassette singles will help give you the edge you need. Run your race to win!

LONELY IN THE MIDST OF A CROWD
Loneliness is a devastating disease. Learn how to trust and count on others to help.

HERBS FOR HEALTH
A look at the concerns and fears of modern medicine. Learn the correct ways to open the doors to your healing.

HOW TO GET ANYTHING YOU WANT
You can learn the way to get anything you want from God!

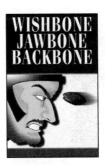

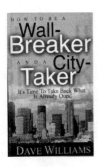

WISHBONE, JAWBONE, BACKBONE
Learn about King David, and how his three "bones" for success can help you in your life quest.

FATAL ENTICEMENTS
Learn how you can avoid the vice-like grip of sin and it's fatal enticements that hold people captive.

HOW TO BE A WALL BREAKER AND A CITY TAKER
You can be a powerful force for advancing the Kingdom of Jesus Christ!

These and other audio tapes available from Dave Williams and:

DECAPOLIS PUBLISHING

Expanding Your Faith

These exciting audio teaching series will help you to grow and mature in your walk with Christ. Get ready for amazing new adventures in faith!

THE BLESSING
Explore the many ways that God can use you to bless others, and how He can correct the missed blessing.

SIN'S GRIP
Learn how you can avoid the vice-like grip of sin and it's fatal enticements that hold people captive.

FAITH, HOPE, & LOVE
Listen and let these three "most important things in life" change you.

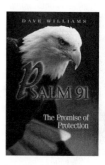

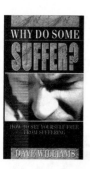

PSALM 91
THE PROMISE OF PROTECTION
Everyone is looking for protection in these perilous times. God promises protection for those who rest in Him.

DEVELOPING
THE SPIRIT OF A CONQUEROR
You can be a conqueror through Christ! Also, find out how to *keep* those things that you have conquered.

WHY DO SOME SUFFER
Find out why some people seem to have suffering in their lives, and find out how to avoid it in your life.

These and other audio tapes available from Dave Williams and:

DECAPOLIS
PUBLISHING

Expanding Your Faith

These exciting audio teaching series will help
you to grow and mature in your walk with Christ.
Get ready for amazing new adventures in faith!

**ABCs OF SUCCESS
AND HAPPINESS**
Learn how to go after God's
promises for your life.
Happiness and success can
be yours today!

FORGIVENESS
The miracle remedy for
many of life's problems is
found in this basic key for
living.

**UNTANGLING YOUR
TROUBLES**
You can be a "trouble
untangler" with the help of
Jesus!

**HOW TO BE A HIGH
PERFORMANCE BELIEVER**
Put in the nine spiritual
additives to help run your
race and get the prize!

**BEING A DISCIPLE AND
MAKING DISCIPLES**
You can learn to be a
"disciple maker" to almost
anyone.

**HOW TO HELP YOUR
PASTOR & CHURCH
SUCCEED**
You can be an integral part
of your church's & pastor's
success.

These and other audio tapes
available from Dave Williams and:

More Products by Dave Williams

BOOK Title	Price
The New Life — The Start Of Something Wonderful	$1.95
End Times Bible Prophecy	$4.95
Seven Sign Posts On the Road To Spiritual Maturity	$4.95
Somebody Out There Needs You	$4.95
Growing Up In Our Father's Family	$4.95
Grief & Mourning	$7.95
The World Beyond — Mysteries Of Heaven	$7.95
The Secret Of Power With God	$7.95
What To Do If You Miss the Rapture	$9.95
Genuine Prosperity	$9.95
The Miracle Results Of Fasting	$9.95
How To Be A High Performance Believer	$9.95
Gifts That Shape Your Life & Change Your World	$10.95
Road To Radical Riches	$19.95

CD Title	Num. of CDs	Price
Middle East Crisis	1	$12.00
Setting Our Houses In Order	1	$12.00
Too Much Baggage?	1	$12.00
Jesus Loves Sinners	1	$12.00
How To Get Your Breakthrough	1	$12.00
Amazing Power Of Desire	1	$12.00
Wounded Spirit	1	$12.00
The Attack On America (Sept. 11, 2001)	1	$12.00
Radical Wealth	5	$60.00

VIDEO Title	Num. of Videos	Price
What To Do When You Are Going Through Hell	1	$19.95
Acres Of Diamonds — The Valley Of Baca	1	$19.95
120 Elite Warriors	1	$19.95
What To Do If You Miss the Rapture	1	$19.95
Regaining Your Spiritual Momentum	1	$19.95
Herbs For Health	1	$19.95
The Destructive Power Of Legalism	1	$19.95
4 Ugly Worms Of Judgment	1	$19.95
Grief and Mourning	1	$19.95
Breaking the Power Of Poverty	1	$19.95
Triple Benefits Of Fasting	1	$19.95
Why Some Are Not Healed	2	$39.95
Miracle Results Of Fasting	3	$59.95
ABCs Of Success and Happiness	3	$59.95
Gifts That Shape Your Life and Change Your World	5	$99.95

AUDIO Title	*Num. of Tapes*	*Price*
Lonely In the Midst Of a Crowd	1	$6.00
How To Get Anything You Want	1	$6.00
Untangling Your Troubles	2	$12.00
Healing Principles In the Ministry Of Jesus	2	$12.00
Acres Of Diamonds — The Valley Of Baca	2	$12.00
Finding Peace	2	$12.00
Criticize & Judge	2	$12.00
Judgment On America	2	$12.00
Triple Benefits Of Fasting	2	$12.00
Global Confusion	2	$12.00
The Cure For a Broken Heart	2	$12.00
Help! I'm Getting Older	2	$12.00
Regaining Your Spiritual Momentum	2	$12.00
The Destructive Power Of Legalism	2	$12.00
Three Most Important Things In Life	3	$18.00
The Final Series	3	$18.00
The Mysteries of Heaven	3	$18.00
Dave Williams' Crash Course In Intercessory Prayer	3	$18.00
Forgiveness — The Miracle Remedy	4	$24.00
How Long Until the End	4	$24.00
What To Do When You Feel Weak and Defeated	4	$24.00
Sin's Grip	4	$24.00
Why Some Are Not Healed	4	$24.00
Bible Cures	4	$24.00
Belial	4	$24.00
God is Closer Than You Think	5	$30.00
Decoding the Apocalypse	5	$30.00
Winning Your Inner Conflict	5	$30.00
Radical Wealth	5	$30.00
Violent Action For Your Wealth	5	$30.00
The Presence Of God	6	$36.00
Your Spectacular Mind	6	$36.00
The Miracle Results of Fasting	6	$36.00
Developing the Spirit Of a Conqueror	6	$36.00
Why Do Some Suffer	6	$36.00
Overcoming Life's Adversities	6	$36.00
Faith Steps	6	$36.00
ABCs For Success & Happiness	6	$36.00
The Best Of Dave Williams	6	$36.00
How To Help Your Pastor & Church Succeed	8	$48.00
Being a Disciple & Making Disciples	8	$48.00
High Performance Believer	8	$48.00
True Or False	8	$48.00
The End Times	8	$48.00
The Beatitudes — Success 101	8	$48.00
Hearing the Voice Of God	10	$60.00
Gifts That Shape Your Life — Personality Gifts	10	$60.00
Gifts That Shape Your Life & Change Your World — Ministry Gifts	10	$60.00
Daniel Parts 1 & 2 (Both parts 6 tapes each)	12	$72.00
Roadblocks To Your Radical Wealth	12	$72.00
Revelation Parts 1 & 2 (part 1 - 6 tapes; part 2 - 8 tapes)	14	$84.00

<u>*Mount Hope Ministries*</u>

Mount Hope Missions & International Outreach
Care Ministries, Deaf Ministries
& Support Groups
Access to Christ for the Physically Impaired
Community Outreach Ministries
Mount Hope Youth Ministries
Mount Hope Bible Training Institute
The Hope Store and Decapolis Publishing
The Pacesetter's Path Telecast
The Pastor's Minute Radio Broadcast
Mount Hope Children's Ministry
Champions Club and Sidewalk Sunday School
The Saturday Care Clinic

When you're facing a struggle and need someone to pray with you, please call us at (517) 321-CARE or (517) 327-PRAY. We have pastors on duty 24 hours a day. We know you hurt sometimes and need a pastor, a minister, or a prayer partner. There will be ministers and prayer partners here for you.

If you'd like to write, we'd be honored to pray for you. Our address is:

MOUNT HOPE CHURCH
202 S. CREYTS RD.
LANSING, MI 48917
(517) 321-CARE or (517) 321-2780
FAX (517)321-6332
TDD (517) 321-8200

www.mounthopechurch.org
email:
mhc@mounthopechurch.org

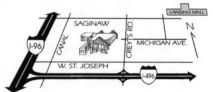

West of the Lansing Mall, on Creyts at Michigan Ave.